11/17

Young
Rewired
State_

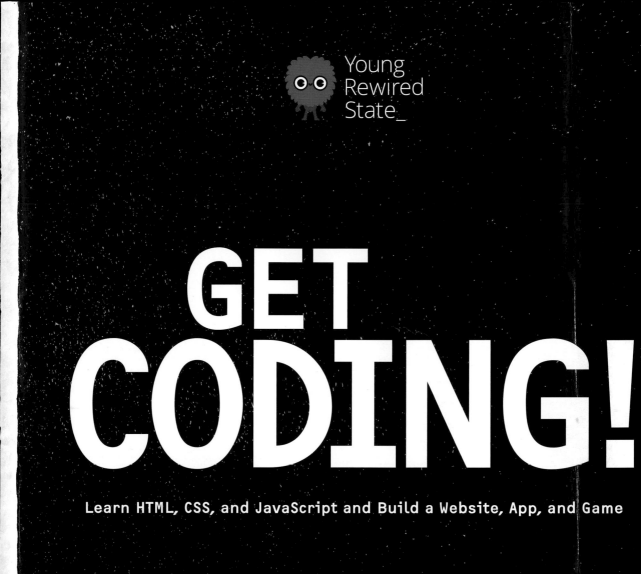

GET CODING!

Learn HTML, CSS, and JavaScript and Build a Website, App, and Game

CANDLEWICK PRESS

CONTENTS

ABOUT THIS BOOK 4

INTRODUCTION 6

HOW TO USE THIS BOOK 12

KEY CODE SKILLS 13

MISSION 1: Build a Web Page 16

MISSION 2: Create a Password 58

MISSION 3: Build an App 94

MISSION 4: Plan a Route 134

MISSION 5: Make a Game 152

MISSION 6: Your Finished Website 188

WHAT NEXT? 204

INDEX 206

ABOUT THIS BOOK

Hello! We're Young Rewired State, a worldwide community of digital makers age eighteen and under. We've made this book because we want you to become a technology star of the future. We hope that *Get Coding!* will not only teach you how to code but also show you how fun and exciting it can be. Coding is one of the most important skills young people can learn, and there's never been a better time to master it.

what does this book teach you?

This book teaches you how to code using three essential programming languages: HTML, CSS, and JavaScript. A computer can be made to do almost anything, but first someone has to write a program for it to follow. Programs have to be written in languages a computer can understand. Coding is all about learning to write programs in these different languages.

HTML, CSS, and JavaScript are three of the most important programming languages in the world. They are used by web developers to build the websites and web-based apps and games you use every day. This book will teach you how to write code and build programs using these programming languages. In this book you will learn real-life coding skills you can use to do all kinds of programming.

Young Rewired State_

Find out more about Young Rewired State:
www.yrs.io   www.getcodingkids.com

Go to
www.getcodingkids.com
for help and support

How does this book work?

There are six chapters in this book. Each chapter contains a mission that will teach you new HTML, CSS, and JavaScript coding skills. Your job is to work through the chapters and use your skills to complete the missions. You will be joining Professor Bairstone, Dr. Day, and Ernest, who need your help to keep a valuable diamond safe.

What do you need?

All you need is a computer (PC or Mac) that is connected to the Internet.

We hope you enjoy this book and that it inspires you to get coding!

Tweet us: **@youngrewired #GetCoding**
Also find us on YouTube, Facebook, and Instagram

INTRODUCTION
COMPUTER CODING

Computers are an important part of our lives today. We use them all the time to do many different things. You've probably used a laptop, desktop computer, or tablet before. But did you know that a smartphone is also a computer? And that there are computers inside ATMs, washing machines, game consoles, and cars? All these computers look different and work slightly differently, but all have one thing in common: they have to follow sets of instructions, called programs, to complete tasks.

Perfect Programming

Computers are electronic devices that can process information. They can be the size of a room or fit inside tiny gadgets, and they do all kinds of complex tasks. Computers are made up of hardware (the physical parts of a computer you can touch) and software (the parts you can't touch). Computers need software because they can't think or act by themselves. They have to follow a detailed series of commands in a piece of software known as a program. Programs are written in programming languages that computers can understand. Writing programs is therefore known as coding or programming. You can write programs to do all sorts of things.

Apps you may have used:

- Facebook
- Google
- iTunes
- Microsoft Word
- Minecraft
- YouTube

You use programs every day. When you check your friend's profile on Facebook, send a text, use a microwave, or play a DVD, you're using computer programs. In fact, you can write a program to make a computer do almost anything. The people who write programs are called programmers or software developers. Programmers write code in different programming languages depending on the type of program they want to build.

Programming Languages

There are many different programming languages you can code in. Computers can understand more than one programming language at a time, so programs are often written using several different programming languages. A programmer's job is to pick the best languages for the program they are building, because different programming languages work better for different things. Every programming language has things it's good and bad at. Some commonly used programming languages are listed below.

- **C** and **C++** are used to build operating systems for your computer.
- **C#, Java, PHP,** and **Ruby** are used to build websites.
- **C#, Java,** and **Objective-C** are used to write **apps** for computers and smartphones.
- **SQL** is used to extract information from databases.

You may have already done some coding at school, using programming languages such as Scratch or Python. Scratch is made up of colored blocks of code that you drag and drop together to create programs. It's great for making small games and animations. Python is a text-based programming language, which means you create programs by typing out each instruction for your computer as a piece of code. Programs like Instagram are written in Python.

In this book you are going to learn how to write code using three programming languages: HTML, CSS, and JavaScript. Using these programming languages, you are going to create programs that run on the Internet. You are going to create a website, app, game, and many other programs that will run in your web browser.

CODE WORDS

An **APP (APPLICATION)** is a type of computer program. Apps are usually programs that a user needs to perform specific tasks, like word processing or e-mailing.

Look at all the different programming languages you can code in!

CODING AND THE WEB

A giant network connects lots of computers all over the world. This network is called the Internet, and it allows us to access and share information with people around the world in seconds. You've probably used the Internet to visit websites, watch videos, send e-mails, listen to music, or play games. But did you know that when you connect to the Internet and view a website, you are using a chain of different computer programs? Programs on our computers called web browsers connect via Internet networks to programs running on web servers, letting us share information quickly and easily.

World Wide Web

The Internet is made up of lots of smaller networks. The World Wide Web (or "the web") is a network connecting many of our computers, used daily by millions of people. The web is made up of lots of individual web pages.

A web page is a file written in computer code by a programmer. Web pages are nearly all written in the same programming language, which is called HTML. HTML contains the information your computer needs to display a web page on-screen. When a group of web pages is linked together, the group of pages is called a website. You access web pages using a program called a web browser.

Web Browsers

Web browsers are computer programs that allow us to view web pages. You have probably come across web browsers such as Google Chrome, Microsoft Internet Explorer, Safari, and Mozilla Firefox, and used them to access all sorts of different websites. Your web browser uses a web address to find the web page you want on the web. It then accesses the information for the web page using another program called a web server.

Professor Bairstone is always online, sending e-mails!

Web Servers

Servers are computers that provide other computers with information. A web server can be either hardware (a computer) or software (a program) ███ ██ to deliver a web page to your browser. To access a web page, your web browser has to connect to that page's web server. The program running on the web server then finds the web page your browser has requested. It then sends the web page to your computer as HTML code.

Web server

Web browser asks for the web page.

Web server sends the web page.

Web browser

Web Addresses

Web addresses, or URLs, as they are more commonly known, are a handy way for a web browser to find the web server and HTML file it needs on the web. There are millions of websites on the Internet, and if each web page didn't have an individual URL, your web browser wouldn't know where to look for it. URLs are split into different parts, each telling your web browser a different piece of information:

This tells the web browser to connect to a web server.

This tells the server to send your web browser an HTML file.

http://www.getcodingkids.com/hello.html

This tells the web browser which server to connect to.

Web Pages

When the web server sends your web browser a web page, it sends the information in an HTML document. HTML documents are made up of HTML elements, such as text and images, as well as exact instructions for the browser about how to display and position the elements on-screen.

When a web browser reads the instructions in the HTML code, we say the browser parses the HTML document. As it parses and decodes the instructions, the browser draws each element of the document on-screen. An HTML document could contain just a few words of text. The simplest HTML document is only a few lines of code long and looks like this:

```html
<!DOCTYPE html>
<html>
<head>                  HTML element
    <title>Get Coding!</title>
</head>
<body>
    Are you ready to get coding?
</body>
</html>
```

Or the document might be more complicated, containing other programming languages as well, such as CSS and JavaScript.

Turn the page to find out more about HTML and the other programming languages used to code web pages!

CODING WEB PAGES

The three most common programming languages in the world are HTML, CSS, and JavaScript. These languages are used to build web pages and web-based apps. Using them together allows you to build web pages that not only look great but are interactive too. In this book you are going to learn how to code in these languages.

HTML

Today, nearly all web pages are written using HTML (HyperText Markup Language) code. HTML was developed by Tim Berners-Lee in the early 1990s. HTML is a great way of creating the basic structure of your web page. HTML documents are made up of individual HTML elements. Elements are created using opening and closing tags. Each tag is the name of the element enclosed in angle brackets (< >). The content goes between the tags. Each HTML tag is an instruction to your web browser, telling it how to show the content on your screen. Tags allow you to add text, images, and videos to your web page and to divide information into sections, such as lines or paragraphs.

CSS

CSS (Cascading Style Sheets) is a programming language that works with HTML to make your web page look good. HTML looks very boring on its own, so you use CSS to change the color, font, and position of text and images. CSS will let you make a piece of text bigger or smaller, change your background color, or position an image in the center of a page.

JavaScript

JavaScript is a very important programming language because it brings web pages to life by making them interactive. An interactive web page changes when the user does something. So if you want your user to be able to click a button, or an alert to pop up, you need to use JavaScript. If you use HTML and CSS without JavaScript, you will have a web page that looks great but doesn't respond to the user.

Some clever coders

Ada Lovelace (1815—1852) wrote the world's first computer program in 1843.

Grace Hopper (1906—1992) created the world's first computer compiler, a program that turns human-readable code into computer code.

Tim Berners-Lee (1955—) is a computer scientist who invented the World Wide Web and the HTML programming language.

Alan Turing (1912—1954) was a mathematician who established the foundations of modern computer science.

Paul Allen (1953—) and **Bill Gates** (1955—) founded the Microsoft technology company and created the Microsoft Windows operating system.

Brendan Eich (1961—) created the JavaScript programming language.

Markus Persson (1979—) is a computer game programmer who created Minecraft.

Sergey Brin (1973—) and **Larry Page** (1973—) are computer scientists and Internet entrepreneurs who cofounded the Google search engine.

Mark Zuckerberg (1984—) is a computer programmer and Internet entrepreneur who cofounded Facebook.

These are very brainy people!

HOW TO USE THIS BOOK

There are six exciting missions in *Get Coding!* Your job is to work through each mission and learn how to code in HTML, CSS, and JavaScript. You can then use your new coding skills to help the intrepid explorer Professor Bairstone and top scientist Dr. Day, who are in urgent need of your assistance. They have found the valuable Monk Diamond on an expedition and need your help to keep it safe.

Mission Briefs

At the start of each mission, you will receive a Mission Brief from Professor Bairstone or Dr. Day. The brief will ask you to use your coding knowledge to help with a Do-It-Yourself Task. The tasks include building a web page, creating a password, coding an app, planning a route, making a game, and building a finished website.

Code Skills

The best way to learn how to code is through practice! At first coding can seem daunting since you have to use special words and symbols. But you will soon become familiar with the ways the different programming languages have to be written. To help you see how each new piece of code works, you will find Code Skills exercises dotted throughout each mission. Follow the step-by-step instructions in each exercise, and master a new Code Skill every time.

The Explorer's Encyclopedia

You will find out more about Professor Bairstone, Dr. Day, and the Monk Diamond in the entries from the Explorer's Encyclopedia after the briefs. You can use this information to help you complete the tasks.

The Monk Diamond

Do-It-Yourself Tasks

At the end of each mission is a Do-It-Yourself Task. Use the code you have learned in the Code Skills to complete the tasks and accomplish the missions. The future of the Monk Diamond is in your hands!

KEY CODE SKILLS

Before you receive the brief for Mission 1, there are some basic Code Skills you need to learn. You will use these skills throughout the entire book, so it's important to get a handle on them now. You can code using a PC or a Mac, but you have to create and save your HTML file in a different way depending on which system you are using.

KEY CODE SKILL 1 ► CREATING A FOLDER

You need to have a place in your computer where you can save all your HTML files. Make a folder on your desktop called **Coding**. It's really important that you save all your HTML files in the same place, so make sure you keep using this folder as you work through the missions.

PC
On a PC, right-click on your desktop and click *New* and then *Folder*. Call your new folder **Coding**.

Mac
On a Mac, hold down the Control key and click on your desktop. Then select *New Folder*. Call your new folder **Coding**.

> Master these essential Code Skills and you'll be ready for the first mission!

KEY CODE SKILL 2 ► CREATING AN HTML FILE

You need to know how to create an HTML file so you can write code. Programmers normally use specialist software to write code, but all computers come with text-editing programs that let you write HTML files. If you have a PC, you can use Notepad. If you have a Mac, you can use TextEdit.

PC

On a PC, you'll find Notepad by going into the *Start* menu and typing it in the search bar.

Mac

On a Mac, you'll find TextEdit by typing it in the *Spotlight* search magnifying glass in the top-right of your screen. When you open TextEdit, you need to do the following things:
- Set up your file as a plain text (rather than rich text) file. To do this, go to *Format* in the menu bar and select *Make Plain Text*.
- Also go to *TextEdit* in the menu bar. Select *Preferences*. In the *New Document* tab in the *Format* section, make sure *Plain text* is checked. In the *Options* section, make sure *Smart quotes* is unchecked.
- In the *Open and Save* tab in *Preferences,* make sure *Display HTML files as HTML code instead of formatted text* is checked.

KEY CODE SKILL 3 ► SAVING YOUR HTML FILE

When you save your HTML file for the first time, you need to make sure you save it using the file extension **.html** at the end of your file name. Your computer uses file extensions to work out how to open files. By giving your file the extension **.html**, you're telling your computer that it should open it in a web browser.

PC

On a PC, you need to:
- Go to *File* and select *Save As*.
- Select the **Coding** folder as the destination to save the file to.
- Choose a name for your file, such as Mission1, and type it into the *File name* bar.
- After the name of the file, type **.html** so your file name reads **Mission1.html**. Click *Save*.

Mac

On a Mac, you need to:
- Go to *File* and select *Save*.
- Select your **Coding** folder as the destination to save your file to.
- Choose a name for your file, such as Mission1, and type it into the *Save As* bar.
- After the name of the file, type **.html** so your file name reads **Mission1.html**.
- Make sure the check box *If no extension is provided, use ".txt".* is unchecked. Click *Save*.

KEY CODE SKILL 4 ► OPENING YOUR HTML FILE

To see your code displayed on-screen, you need to open your HTML file in a web browser. You then might want to go back into your text-editing program to make some changes to your code.

PC

On a PC, you need to:
- Save your file, as described in Key Code Skill 3.
- Open your **Coding** folder on your desktop. Double-click on your HTML file. It will open in your web browser.
- When you want to edit your code, right-click on the HTML file in your **Coding** folder. Select *Open with* and choose Notepad.

Mac

On a Mac, you need to:
- Save your file, as described in Key Code Skill 3.
- Open your **Coding** folder on your desktop. Double-click on your HTML file. It will open in your web browser.
- When you want to edit your code, right-click on the HTML file in your **Coding** folder. Select *Open with* and choose TextEdit.

> Use a web browser like Mozilla Firefox or Google Chrome.

KEY CODE SKILL 5 ► USING THE *GET CODING!* WEBSITE

Don't forget that as you work through the book, you can use the *Get Coding!* website to help you with your missions. You'll find entries from the Explorer's Encyclopedia and images that you can use. If you get stuck at any point when you're writing code, go to the website and see what your code block should look like. You can even copy and paste the code blocks from the website into your text-editing program.

The *Get Coding!* URL is **www.getcodingkids.com**.

On the website you will find:
- Professor Bairstone's entries on the Explorer's Encyclopedia
- Pictures of Professor Bairstone, Ernest, Dr. Day, and the Monk Diamond
- Code blocks for each Code Skills exercise and Do-It-Yourself Task

> Some of these steps may vary depending on the system you're using. If you're having trouble, do an online search for how to write HTML in the version of the program you're using.

Mission 1

BUILD A WEB PAGE

- ◆ LEARN WHAT HTML IS AND HOW IT WORKS

- ◆ MAKE A SIMPLE WEB PAGE USING HTML

- ◆ ADD TEXT AND IMAGES TO YOUR HTML WEB PAGE

- ◆ LEARN HOW TO LAY OUT AND DESIGN YOUR WEB PAGE USING CSS

Dear Coder,

We haven't met before, but I'm sure you already know my name. I'm the famous explorer Professor Harry Bairstone. I'm e-mailing you because I am in desperate need of your help.

I am currently on an expedition in the mountains of Siberia, with the top scientist Dr. Ruby Day and my dog, Ernest. The aim of our expedition was to find prehistoric fossils. Instead we have made an even more sensational discovery.

We were exploring a cave when Ernest suddenly started barking and sniffing at a large boulder. We looked closer and saw that something had been hidden in a crack in the rock face. Dr. Day pulled out the object. It was a small box wrapped in oilcloth. When I opened the box, I couldn't believe my eyes.

It was the legendary Monk Diamond! As I'm sure you know, the Monk Diamond was stolen from Moscow three years ago in a daring robbery, and its whereabouts have been unknown until now. Our discovery is of great international significance.

We can only access the Internet briefly, using my emergency booster pack. Dr. Day and I were hoping you could help us by using your Code Skills to build a web page about our exciting discovery.

I'm attaching an entry from the Explorer's Encyclopedia, which will tell you all about the Monk Diamond's remarkable history. You can use the information to build your web page. We will use the page to announce our discovery to the world the moment we arrive in Moscow.

Thank you for helping us with this exciting mission. It's going to be great!

Warmest wishes from the chilly mountains,
Professor Harry Bairstone

THE EXPLORER'S
ENCYCLOPEDIA
The Guide to Every Adventure

Home page
Contents
Featured discoveries
Famous explorers
Historical expeditions

The Monk Diamond

From the Explorer's Encyclopedia: The Guide to Every Adventure

This entry is about the Monk Diamond. For other jewels, see <u>Jewels</u>.

The **Monk Diamond** is one of the rarest and most precious <u>diamonds</u> in the world, famous for its distinctive green color. It was discovered in 1880 and was bought by a Russian nobleman for his wife in 1889.

During the <u>Russian Revolution</u>, the Monk Diamond was stolen from the nobleman's palace in <u>St. Petersburg</u>. For the next thirty years, the Monk Diamond's whereabouts

Professor Bairstone's Fact File

The Monk Diamond

Age:	over 1 billion years old
Color:	Green
Cut:	Oval
Carats:	300
Clarity:	Flawless
Value:	over $10 million

were unknown. In 1947 it was found during a police raid on a gang of petty criminals in Moscow and returned to the nobleman's family.

The nobleman's son decided the Monk Diamond was unlucky and sold it to the House of Volkov, Moscow's oldest jewelry store. The House of Volkov paid an undisclosed sum for the jewel, but it was rumored to be the most expensive diamond sale ever.

The Monk Diamond was on display in the House of Volkov's private collection until three years ago, when it was stolen in an audacious raid. Despite a long investigation and the promise of a huge reward, the police were unable to track down the culprits, and the case remains unsolved.

The thieves are believed to be the Bond Brothers, the international gang of jewel thieves responsible for numerous high-profile thefts. A theory put forward by the explorer Professor Bairstone is that the Monk Diamond was smuggled out of Moscow by the Bond Brothers and hidden somewhere in Russia. He thinks "the thieves are biding their time until they can sell the diamond on the black market without attracting suspicion."

CODING WITH HTML

Now that you've read the Mission Brief, it's time to get coding. To build Professor Bairstone's web page, you're first going to need to learn to write HTML (HyperText Markup Language). HTML is the programming language used by programmers to build websites. It allows you to give your browser instructions. You use HTML to add text and images to a web page. You also use it to group pieces of information into lines, paragraphs, or sections.

An HTML web page is called a document. It's made up of HTML elements. Elements are created using small pieces of code called tags. Tags nearly always come in pairs and surround every piece of content (like a piece of text or an image) on the page. Each tag contains an instruction for your web browser, telling it how to show the element on-screen. This is why HTML is called a markup language. You use tags to mark up each piece of content with an instruction for your browser.

HTML Tags

Each tag is made up of a piece of code surrounded by two angle brackets (< >). The angle brackets are on the same keys as the period and comma symbols on your keyboard. Let's look at an example of a tag:

> It's simple: <p> is code for paragraph. You'll learn more about this tag later in the mission.

```
<p>Professor Bairstone and Dr. Day have discovered the Monk Diamond.</p>
```

opening tag

closing tag

This is the paragraph <p> tag. When tags come in pairs, we call the first tag the opening tag and the second tag the closing tag. You can spot a closing tag because it contains a forward slash (/). When your browser reads this code, it understands that you are telling it to group the text between the opening and closing <p> tags into a paragraph.

To code a web page, you have to create an HTML file in a text-editing program. Your browser expects some tags to appear in a certain order. You need to code the tags that contain instructions about the whole page first. Then you code the tags with instructions for specific pieces of content on your page. Tags can be put inside other tags. You just have to remember to close each tag when you've finished with it.

Let's look at the HTML tags you need to code a very simple web page. If you use these tags, you will create a web page that is made up of a title and some text. Each tag gives your browser a different piece of information:

`<!DOCTYPE html>`

This is called the <!DOCTYPE> declaration, and it is always the first line of an HTML file. It tells our browser what version of HTML our page has been coded in. It is not an HTML tag so it is written with capital letters, and it doesn't need a closing tag.

`<html>`

This is the <html> tag, and it tells the browser that we have used HTML to code our page.

```
<!DOCTYPE html>
<html>
<head>
    <title>
        The Monk Diamond Discovery
    </title>
</head>
<body>
    <p>Professor Bairstone and Dr. Day have
        discovered the Monk Diamond.</p>
</body>
</html>
```

`<title>`

The <title> tag goes inside the <head> tag. The content between the tags will not appear in the main body of our page. It will be the title of the browser window when you open the page in your browser.

`<head>`

This is the <head> tag. Inside are pieces of content that aren't displayed in the main <body> of your page, like the title. You can also put instructions that you want your browser to apply to your whole page here.

`<body>`

All the content you want to see displayed in your web page goes inside the <body> tag. So this text about the Monk Diamond will appear on our page when we open the file in our web browser.

`<p>`

This is the paragraph tag. All the text between the opening and closing tags will be grouped into a paragraph.

Turn the page to see what this code will look like on-screen in our web browser!

21

When we save the code we wrote in our text-editing program and then open it in our web browser, our browser decodes our HTML file and draws on-screen a web page that looks like this:

The Monk Diamond Di ✖

Professor Bairstone and Dr. Day have discovered the Monk Diamond.

See how the text between the opening and closing `<title>` tags has become the title of the browser window?

Look at how all the text between the opening and closing `<p>` tags has become the content of your web page!

Writing HTML

Now that you know what HTML tags are and how they work, it's time for you to try using them. The best way to learn new pieces of code is to practice writing them. Throughout this book you will find Code Skills. Follow the step-by-step instructions in the exercises and learn new skills each time.

It's really important to make sure your code is as accurate as possible. Having a letter or a symbol wrong or missing could stop your code from working, as your browser won't be able to understand your instructions. If you are having problems making a program work, it's a good idea to check the following things:

- ♥ That you haven't missed any tags or used them in the wrong order
- ♥ That there are no typos or spelling errors in your code
- ♥ That you've used correct capitalization throughout your code
- ♥ That you've included all the symbols you need, in the right order
- ♥ That you're using straight quotes (" ") and not curly quotes (" ")
- ♥ That you've closed all your tags by including the forward slash (/)
- ♥ That your text-editing program has saved your file as an HTML file (**.html**)

These are some top tips for writing code!

If you're still stuck, go to the *Get Coding!* website (**www.getcodingkids.com**), where you will be able to copy and paste the code block you need.

CODE SKILLS ▶ WRITING HTML

Let's use HTML tags to code a very simple web page. Follow these steps to learn how to structure an HTML web page that is made up of a title and a piece of text.

1. Open up your text-editing program. Look back at Key Code Skill 2 on page 14 if you need a reminder about how to do this.

2. Type this code into your text-editing program:

```
<!DOCTYPE html>
<html>
<head>
    <title>The Monk Diamond</title>
</head>
<body>
    <p>The Monk Diamond is a rare jewel.</p>
</body>
</html>
```

Make sure you copy the code carefully. Your web browser won't be able to read your code if there are any mistakes in it. The <!DOCTYPE> declaration has to have capital letters, and your last tag always has to be </html>. Check that you have closed each tag by including the forward slash (/).

3. Save your file in your **Coding** folder as an HTML file (**.html**). Call it **webpagetemplate.html**. Go back to Key Code Skills 1 and 3 on pages 13 and 14 if you need a reminder about how to do this.

4. Open your HTML file in your web browser. See Key Code Skill 4 on page 15 if you need a reminder about how to do this. Your code will be displayed on-screen as a web page, like this:

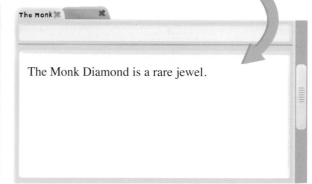

The Monk Diamond is a rare jewel.

Then open your file in your text-editing program again. Change the text between the opening and closing <title> tags and <p> tags to text of your choice. Save your file.

5. Click the *Refresh* button in your browser, or press F5 on a PC or Command+R on a Mac. Your changes to the text will appear on-screen.

You just built your first web page!

BUILDING A WEB PAGE WITH HTML TAGS

Now that you can write HTML tags, let's look at how we can use them to code a more complex web page. As you've just seen in the Code Skill on the previous page, if you write text between the opening and closing <p> tags, it will appear on-screen. But just having one block of text on our web page won't look very exciting. If we want to make new lines or paragraphs, we have to learn new tags.

We need to put these new tags between our opening and closing <body> tags. Putting tags inside other tags is called nesting. Nesting tags allows us to create more exciting page layouts. Let's look at an example of nesting with the <body> tag and the paragraph <p> tag:

```
<body>
    <p>The Monk Diamond is worth over $10 million.</p>
</body>
```

indent

The <p> tag is nested inside the <body> tag.

White space around your HTML doesn't matter. But programmers like to indent their code every time they open a new tag. It helps them keep track of when they've opened and closed a tag and makes the code block easier to read. To indent, press Tab every time you open a new tag.

Let's learn about the tags you need to make paragraphs and line breaks. The code in the tags is very simple. It's just a shorter way of saying "paragraph" and "break."

Did you notice?

All our tags are written in lowercase letters, and there are no spaces between the tags and text.

The Paragraph Tag: <p> and </p>

The paragraph <p> tag lets you make new paragraphs. The opening tag is <p> and the closing tag is </p>. Everything between the opening and closing <p> tags is grouped together. Use a new <p> tag every time you want a new paragraph. Look at this example, where we've coded two paragraphs:

```
<body>
    <p>Professor Bairstone and Dr. Day have made a sensational discovery.</p>
    <p>They have discovered the Monk Diamond in a remote cave in Siberia.</p>
</body>
```

opening paragraph tag

closing paragraph tag

When we open this code in our web browser, it looks like this!

Professor Bairstone and Dr. Day have made a sensational discovery.

They have discovered the Monk Diamond in a remote cave in Siberia.

The Line Break Tag:

The line break <br/> tag lets you start your text on a new line, but without starting a new paragraph. The line break tag is a **self-closing** HTML tag. Because there is no content to display on-screen, the line break tag is a single tag. In this example, we've used both the <p> tag and <br/> tag to change the way our text displays:

```
<body>
   <p>Professor Bairstone and Dr. Day have made a sensational discovery.<br/>
      Professor Bairstone is the world's leading explorer.<br/>
      Dr. Day is a scientist who studies fossils.</p>
   <p>They have discovered the Monk Diamond in a remote cave in Siberia.</p>
</body>
```

line break tag

CODE WORDS

A **SELF-CLOSING** HTML tag is an opening and closing tag rolled into one. Only some kinds of tag are used this way. You can spot a self-closing tag because the forward slash (/) comes at the end of the tag, rather than at the beginning as it does for a regular closing tag.

Professor Bairstone and Dr. Day have made a sensational discovery.
Professor Bairstone is the world's leading explorer.
Dr. Day is a scientist who studies fossils.

They have discovered the Monk Diamond in a remote cave in Siberia.

Now it's time for you to try using these new tags!

25

CODE SKILLS ► CODING PARAGRAPHS AND LINE BREAKS

Let's try coding paragraphs and line breaks in a web page, using the `<p>` and `<br/>` tags.

1. Open up your text-editing program. Create a new HTML file called **breaks.html**. Check the Key Code Skills on pages 13–15 if you need a reminder about how to do this. Then copy and paste your code from **webpagetemplate.html** into your new file. Modify the code so that it looks like this:

```
<!DOCTYPE html>
<html>
<head>
    <title>The Monk Diamond</title>
</head>
<body>
</body>
</html>
```

2. Use the paragraph `<p>` tag. Open the `<p>` tag, type some text, then use the closing `</p>` tag. Repeat as many times as you want. Your code will look like this:

```
<body>
   <p>The Monk Diamond has been
      discovered in Siberia.</p>
   <p>Ernest, Professor Bairstone's
      dog, found the jewel.</p>
</body>
```

3. Type some more text in your first paragraph. Add the line break `<br/>` tag to the end of a line of text, like this:

```
<body>
   <p>The Monk Diamond has been
      discovered in Siberia.<br/>
      Professor Bairstone
      and Dr. Day were on a fossil-
      finding expedition.</p>
   <p>Ernest, Professor Bairstone's
      dog, found the jewel.</p>
</body>
```

4. Save your HTML file in your **Coding** folder. Then open your web page in your browser. Your page will look like this:

The Monk Diamond has been discovered in Siberia.
Professor Bairstone and Dr. Day were on a fossil-finding expedition.

Ernest, Professor Bairstone's dog, found the jewel.

Great work! But what about some pictures of the Monk Diamond?

I think it's time to learn about the image tag!

26

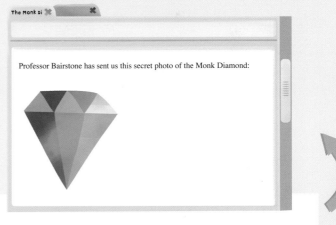

The Image Tag: <img/>

Now that you've mastered the paragraph and line break tags, let's learn how to add an image to our web page. The image <img/> tag is another self-closing tag. Inside the tag itself you have to include a piece of information called the source (src) **attribute**. An image tag looks like this:

```
<img src="image.jpg"/>
```

The equals sign (=) and double quotes (" ") set the value of the source attribute.

You have to include the source attribute in the <img/> tag so your browser knows where to find your image. Without it your browser won't know what to display on-screen. The value of your source attribute can be set to either a file name of a saved image or a URL (web address) of your image.

CODE WORDS

An **ATTRIBUTE** is a useful way of giving your browser extra information about an HTML element. There are lots of different kinds of attributes you can include in your tags.

There are two parts to an attribute: the attribute name and the value of the attribute. You use an equals sign (=) to set the value of the attribute and put the value in double quotes (" "). So an attribute will always look like this: name="value". Attributes are added to the opening tag, or to the only tag (in the case of a self-closing tag).

Using a Saved Image

If you have an image saved as a JPEG file (**.jpg**) in your **Coding** folder, it's really easy to add this image to your page. All you need to do is set the value of the source attribute to the name of your image file, using the equals sign (=) and double quotes (" "). So if your file is called **diamond.jpg**, your code will look like this:

```
<body>
    <p>Professor Bairstone has sent us this secret photo of the Monk Diamond:</p>
    <img src="diamond.jpg"/>
</body>
```

image tag

source attribute

file name

Using an Image URL

If there's an image on the Internet that you want to use on your web page, you have to set the value of the source attribute in your `<img/>` tag to the URL of the image. You find the URL of a picture by right-clicking on it and selecting *Copy image URL* on a PC or *Copy image address* on a Mac. You then paste the URL inside your `<img/>` tag as the value of the source attribute. Don't forget to put it in double quotes (" "), like this:

```
<body>
    <p>This is Professor Bairstone and Dr. Day's first expedition together.</p>
    <p>Here is a photo of the team:</p>
    <img src="https://getcodingkids.com/team_photo.jpg"/>
</body>
```

A URL will always start with http:// or https://

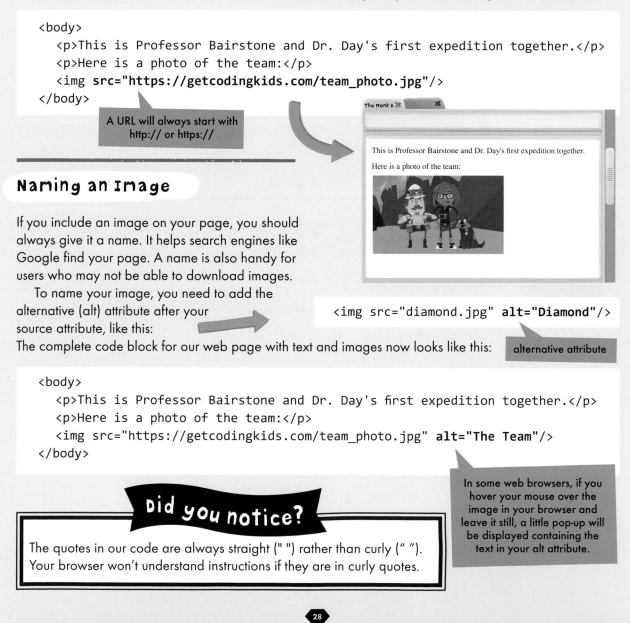

This is Professor Bairstone and Dr. Day's first expedition together.

Here is a photo of the team:

Naming an Image

If you include an image on your page, you should always give it a name. It helps search engines like Google find your page. A name is also handy for users who may not be able to download images.

To name your image, you need to add the alternative (alt) attribute after your source attribute, like this:

```
<img src="diamond.jpg" alt="Diamond"/>
```

alternative attribute

The complete code block for our web page with text and images now looks like this:

```
<body>
    <p>This is Professor Bairstone and Dr. Day's first expedition together.</p>
    <p>Here is a photo of the team:</p>
    <img src="https://getcodingkids.com/team_photo.jpg" alt="The Team"/>
</body>
```

In some web browsers, if you hover your mouse over the image in your browser and leave it still, a little pop-up will be displayed containing the text in your alt attribute.

Did you notice?

The quotes in our code are always straight (" ") rather than curly (" "). Your browser won't understand instructions if they are in curly quotes.

CODE SKILLS ► ADDING IMAGES

Let's try adding some images of the Monk Diamond, Professor Bairstone, Dr. Day, and Ernest to our web page to make it look more exciting.

1. Go to the images section of the *Get Coding!* website. Find the image of the Monk Diamond. Right-click on the image and select *Save Image As*. Save the image as a JPEG file (**.jpg**) in your **Coding** folder. Call it **diamond.jpg**.

2. Open up your text-editing program and create a new HTML file called **images.html**. Then copy and paste your code from **webpagetemplate.html** into your new file. Modify the code so that it looks like this:

```
<!DOCTYPE html>
<html>
<head>
   <title>The Monk Diamond</title>
</head>
<body>
   <p>The Monk Diamond is a rare
      green color.</p>
</body>
</html>
```

3. Now add an image of the Monk Diamond to your page. Add an `<img/>` tag with an empty source attribute after your closing `</p>` tag, like this:

```
<p>The Monk Diamond is a rare green
   color.</p>
<img src=" "/>
```

4. Then add a value to the source attribute. Add the name of the image file you saved in your **Coding** folder, like this:

```
<p>The Monk Diamond is a rare green
   color.</p>
<img src="diamond.jpg"/>
```

 Save your HTML file and open it in your browser. Your image will be displayed on-screen.

5. Now add an image of Professor Bairstone, Dr. Day, and Ernest to your page using a URL. Add another paragraph and an `<img/>` tag with an empty source attribute, like this:

```
<p>The Monk Diamond is a rare green
   color.</p>
<img src="diamond.jpg"/>
<p>The team was delighted with their
   discovery.</p>
<img src=" "/>
```

Don't forget that attributes always have to be in double quotes.

29

6. Go to the images section of the *Get Coding!* website. Find the photo of the team. Right-click and select *Copy image URL* or *Copy image address* depending on your system. Paste the URL into your source attribute, like this:

```
<p>The team was delighted with their discovery.</p>
<img src="https://getcodingkids.com/team_photo.jpg"/>
```

 Save your file and refresh the page in your browser. You will see your second image displayed on-screen.

7. Finally, you need to add two alt attributes to your `<img/>` tags. Choose a name for each of your images. Your code will look like this:

```
<!DOCTYPE html>
<html>
<head>
    <title>The Monk Diamond</title>
</head>
<body>
    <p>The Monk Diamond is a rare green color.</p>
    <img src="diamond.jpg" alt="The Monk Diamond"/>
    <p>The team was delighted with their discovery.</p>
    <img src="https://getcodingkids.com/team_photo.jpg" alt="The Team"/>
</body>
</html>
```

 Save your file and refresh your page. Depending on your browser, you may see the text in the alt attributes if you hover your mouse over the images.

Doesn't Ernest look proud of himself?

CODING WITH HTML

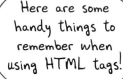

Here are some handy things to remember when using HTML tags!

- The basic structure of an HTML document always looks the same:

- HTML documents are made up of HTML elements. Elements are pieces of content surrounded by HTML tags. Each tag is an instruction to your browser, telling it how to display the content between the opening and closing tags on-screen.

```
<!DOCTYPE html>
<html>
    <head>
    </head>
    <body>
    </body>
</html>
```

- HTML tags are written inside angle brackets (< >). You have an opening and closing tag so your browser knows when the instruction starts and stops. You can always spot a closing tag because it contains a forward slash (/). If there is no content to put between two tags, you use a self-closing tag, which is an opening and closing tag rolled into one.

- Tags are always written in lowercase.

- You can nest HTML tags inside each other. Just don't forget to close your tags.

- When you open a new tag, you should always indent your code by pressing Tab. This makes it easier to read your code.

- If you want to give your browser extra instructions or information about an HTML element, you can use various HTML attributes. Attributes go inside the opening tag. They always have a name and a value, which you set using the equals sign (=) and double quotes (" ").

Web pages normally have more than just words and pictures on them. Turn the page to find out how to change the layout and design of your page.

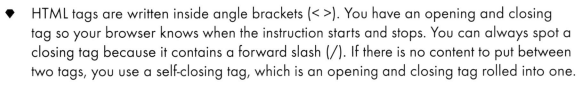

THE LAYOUT AND DESIGN OF YOUR WEB PAGE

Now that you know what HTML tags are and how they work, it's time to start thinking about the layout and design of your web page. So far our HTML elements have been positioned in the same place on our page. If we want to position our text and images in different places or change the design of our web page, we need to learn some new HTML tags and attributes.

The Division Tag: `<div>` and `</div>`

The division `<div>` tag helps us change the layout of a web page by splitting it into sections. The opening tag is `<div>` and the closing tag is `</div>`. The tag is a useful and time-saving way of grouping HTML elements. It works like an invisible container.

When you group HTML elements between an opening and closing `<div>` tag, you can ask your browser to make the same changes to all the elements inside the `<div>`. The elements outside the `<div>` will be unchanged. Let's take a look at how the `<div>` tag works:

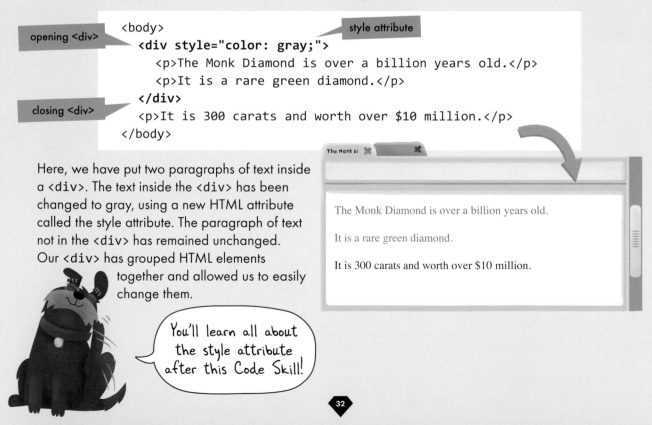

opening `<div>`   style attribute

closing `<div>`

```
<body>
    <div style="color: gray;">
        <p>The Monk Diamond is over a billion years old.</p>
        <p>It is a rare green diamond.</p>
    </div>
    <p>It is 300 carats and worth over $10 million.</p>
</body>
```

The Monk Diamond is over a billion years old.

It is a rare green diamond.

It is 300 carats and worth over $10 million.

Here, we have put two paragraphs of text inside a `<div>`. The text inside the `<div>` has been changed to gray, using a new HTML attribute called the style attribute. The paragraph of text not in the `<div>` has remained unchanged. Our `<div>` has grouped HTML elements together and allowed us to easily change them.

You'll learn all about the style attribute after this Code Skill!

CODE SKILLS ► CREATING SECTIONS

Now it's time for you to try using the `<div>` tag. Master this skill, and you'll be able to make a web page with an interesting layout.

1. Open up your text-editing program. Create a new HTML file called **divs.html**. Then copy and paste your code from **webpagetemplate.html** into your new file. Modify the code so that it looks like this:

```
<!DOCTYPE html>
<html>
<head>
    <title>The Monk Diamond</title>
</head>
<body>
    <p>Professor Bairstone is a famous explorer.</p>
    <p>Dr. Day is a top scientist. She loves dinosaur fossils.</p>
</body>
</html>
```

2. Now add two `<div>` tags between the opening and closing `<body>` tags. Put each paragraph inside a `<div>`, like this:

```
<body>
  <div>
     <p>Professor Bairstone is a famous
        explorer.</p>
  </div>
  <div>
     <p>Dr. Day is a top scientist. She
        loves dinosaur fossils.</p>
  </div>
</body>
```

3. Save your HTML file and open it in your browser. Your `<div>` tags won't have changed anything on-screen, but your elements will be grouped together, ready for you to design and position.

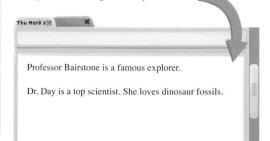

CODING WITH CSS

So far in this mission, you've been coding using HTML. As you've just seen, `<div>` tags are used to group HTML elements so you can easily change them. Next, to change the look and position of your HTML elements, you have to use CSS.

CSS is a programming language often used with HTML. It is used by programmers to change the way HTML elements look when they're displayed in your browser. CSS is short for "Cascading Style Sheets" and is sometimes called style sheets or styles. You can use CSS to change the design of your page by adding colors or changing the size and shape of HTML elements. You can also use CSS to change where things are positioned. In fact, there are many different things you can do with CSS to change the look and feel of your page.

The Style Attribute

To use CSS to change an HTML element, you can add a style attribute to your opening HTML tag. You can use the style attribute with any HTML tag. The style attribute works in exactly the same way as the source and alt attributes we used earlier in the mission. Let's look at how we add a style attribute:

```
<p style="CSS-property: value;">The Monk Diamond had been hidden in a cave.</p>
```

 style attribute CSS

Just like we saw earlier, the value of our style attribute is set using the equals sign (=) and enclosed in double quotes (" "). We apply CSS to our HTML tag by setting the value of the style attribute to CSS. CSS is a very simple programming language to write. It's always split into two parts: a property and a value.

CSS Properties and Values

When you write CSS, you always have to use both a property and a value. The property tells your browser what part of the HTML element you want to change. The value tells your browser exactly what to change it to. So it works like this:

CSS	What does it mean?	Example values
property	The thing you want to change	background-color, height
value	What you want to change it to	red, 200px

When you use CSS, you divide the property from the value by inserting a colon (:). At the end of the value, you use a semicolon (;). If the CSS property name is more than one word, you join the two words using a hyphen (-). If you don't use the right **syntax**, your browser won't be able to decode your instructions. Your style attribute should always be written like this:

```
style="CSS-property: value;"
```

hyphen | colon | semicolon

CODE WORDS

SYNTAX is the set of rules that decides the way a programming language is structured and written.

Your browser has hundreds of different built-in CSS properties and values that you can use in your HTML tags to change your page.

Let's take a closer look at how we can use CSS with <div> tags. If we want to change the background color of a section of our page, we can use CSS and HTML like this:

Look at how we can use HTML and CSS together to change our page!

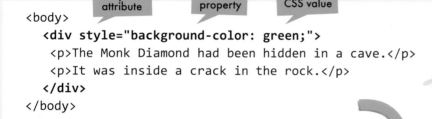

style attribute | CSS property | CSS value

```
<body>
    <div style="background-color: green;">
    <p>The Monk Diamond had been hidden in a cave.</p>
    <p>It was inside a crack in the rock.</p>
    </div>
</body>
```

Did you notice?

It's very important to use not only the right syntax but also the right spelling of the CSS properties and values. Even errors that seem small can prevent your browser from understanding your CSS.

The Monk Di

The Monk Diamond had been hidden in a cave.

It was inside a crack in the rock.

The background-color CSS Property

Now that you understand more about CSS and how it works, let's see how we can use CSS properties to make our page more colorful. Professor Bairstone and Dr. Day's discovery is sure to be an international sensation, and our web page needs to look eye-catching and interesting.

We can change the background color of different areas of our page using different `<div>` tags. First we have to add style attributes to each of our opening `<div>` tags. Then inside the style attribute we set the background-color CSS property and choose a color for the CSS value. The code we need looks like this:

```
<body>
    <p>THE STOLEN MONK DIAMOND IS DISCOVERED!</p>
    <div style="background-color: green;">
        <p>Professor Bairstone, Dr. Day, and Ernest were on an expedition.<br/>
            They made an exciting discovery in the mountains.</p>
    </div>
    <div style="background-color: cyan;">
        <p>Ernest started sniffing and barking at a rock in a cave.<br/>
            Hidden inside the rock was the Monk Diamond.</p>
    </div>
</body>
```

background-color property

This is such a good Code Skill to learn.

The Monk Di

THE STOLEN MONK DIAMOND IS DISCOVERED!

Professor Bairstone, Dr. Day, and Ernest were on an expedition.
They made an exciting discovery in the mountains.

Ernest started sniffing and barking at a rock in a cave.
Hidden inside the rock was the Monk Diamond.

Did you notice?

There are thousands of colors you can use as values in CSS. Go to www.w3schools.com/cssref/css_colornames.asp to view more of them.

 ► WRITING CSS

It's time for you to start using CSS with HTML. Try adding the style attribute to an HTML tag and then setting a CSS property and value.

1. Open up your text-editing program and create a new HTML file called **CSS.html**. Then copy and paste your code from **divs.html** into your new file. Modify the code so that it looks like this:

```
<!DOCTYPE html>
<html>
<head>
   <title>The Monk Diamond</title>
</head>
<body>
   <div>
      <p>The jewel was stolen from Moscow.</p>
      <p>The theft happened three years ago.</p>
   </div>
   <div>
      <p>The Bond Brothers are the prime suspects.</p>
   </div>
</body>
</html>
```

2. Now add an empty style attribute to each of your opening <div> tags, like this:

```
<div style=" ">
```

3. Then add the background-color CSS property to the style attributes. Remember, you need to separate the property name and the value with a colon (:). Don't forget the semicolon (;) at the end of the value. Your opening <div> tags will look like this:

```
<div style="background-color: pink;">
```

4. Save your HTML file and open it in your browser. Try changing the value of the background-color CSS property to different colors. Save your file and refresh your page to see your changes on-screen.

The Monk Di

The jewel was stolen from Moscow.

The theft happened three years ago.

The Bond Brothers are the prime suspects.

MORE CSS PROPERTIES

Let's look at some of the CSS properties we can add to our HTML elements to make Professor Bairstone's web page more exciting. As you know already, CSS is always made up of a property and a value. There are hundreds of different CSS properties and values, but here are some of the most common:

CSS property name	What does it do?	Example values
background-color	Sets the color of your background	red, black, white, yellow
color	Sets the color of your text	red, black, white, yellow
text-align	Positions your text around the page	left, right, center
font-size	Changes the size of your text	12px, 20pt
float	Positions your element to the left or the right of another element	left, right, none
height	Sets the height of your element	100px, 100%
width	Sets the width of your element	100px, 100%
border	Gives your element a border	1px solid black
margin	Adds space around your element	10px
padding	Adds space inside your element	10px

 CODE WORDS Graphics on your computer screen are made up of tiny colored dots called **PIXELS** (px). You can tell your browser how many pixels you want to be in an HTML element.

The color CSS Property

To change the color of your text, use the color CSS property and then choose a value. It's the same as using the background-color property.

 color property

```
<body>
  <div style="color: gray;">The Monk Diamond Discovery!</div>
</body>
```

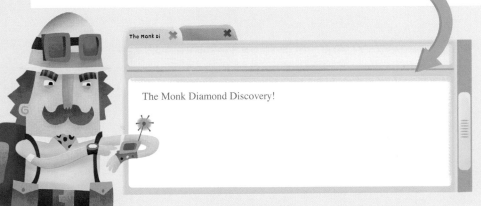

The Monk Diamond Discovery!

Alignment CSS Properties

So far all our HTML elements have been in the same position on our page. The text-align and float CSS properties allow you to align (or position) text and other HTML elements on your page.

The text-align property lets you position your text to the left, right, or center of your page. Remember to include the hyphen (-).

text-align property

```
<body>
  <div style="text-align: center;">
    The Monk Diamond Discovery!
  </div>
  <p>Stolen jewel found in Siberia.</p>
</body>
```

The Monk Diamond Discovery!

Stolen jewel found in Siberia.

We can also use CSS to position HTML elements, such as `<div>` tags or images, to the left or right of the page. You use the float CSS property and set the value to the left or right.

float property

```
<body>
  <div style="float: right;">
    The expedition team:<br/>
    <img src="team.jpg" alt="The Team"/>
  </div>
</body>
```

> The text-align and float CSS properties are easy ways to create an interesting layout for your web page.

The Monk

The expedition team:

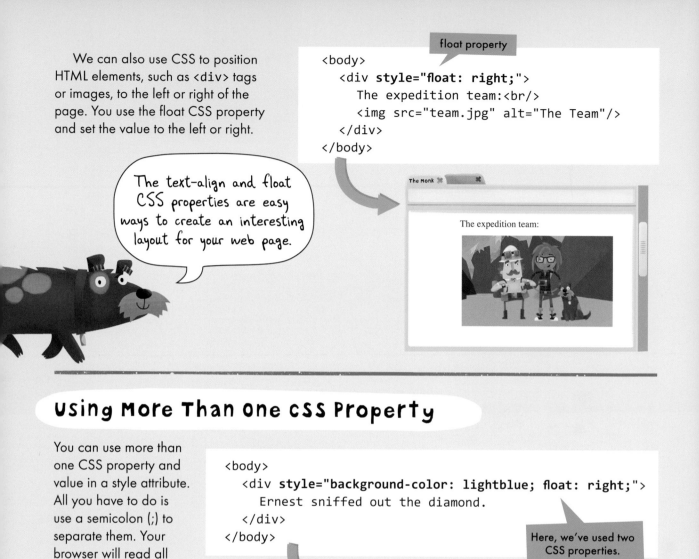

Using More Than One CSS Property

You can use more than one CSS property and value in a style attribute. All you have to do is use a semicolon (;) to separate them. Your browser will read all the CSS properties and apply them to your HTML element, so you can use as many as you need.

```
<body>
  <div style="background-color: lightblue; float: right;">
    Ernest sniffed out the diamond.
  </div>
</body>
```

Here, we've used two CSS properties.

The Monk D

Ernest sniffed out the diamond.

> Look at how we can change both the background color and position of a `<div>`!

40

Making Things Different Sizes with CSS

We now know how to change the color of our text, add background colors to our HTML elements, and position them in different places on the page. But if we want to make a really interesting web page, we also need to know how to change the sizes of our HTML elements. CSS lets us change the size of things really easily. We have to use the width and height CSS properties and set the values to the measurements we want. Let's look at how we can use these properties to make a square `<div>`:

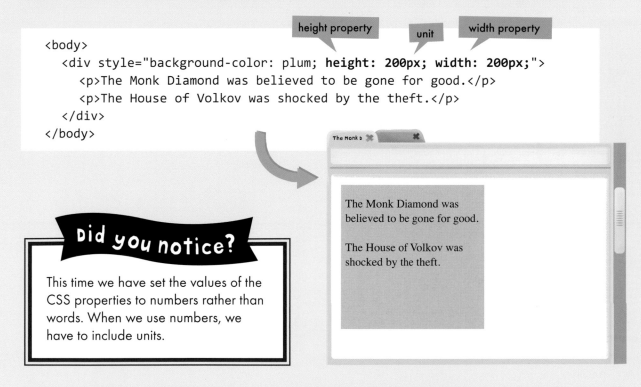

```
<body>
    <div style="background-color: plum; height: 200px; width: 200px;">
        <p>The Monk Diamond was believed to be gone for good.</p>
        <p>The House of Volkov was shocked by the theft.</p>
    </div>
</body>
```

height property · unit · width property

The Monk Diamond was believed to be gone for good.

The House of Volkov was shocked by the theft.

Did you notice?

This time we have set the values of the CSS properties to numbers rather than words. When we use numbers, we have to include units.

Measurements in CSS

There are lots of different units you can use for measuring in CSS. Make sure you tell your browser what unit you are using by typing it after the number value. Here are some of the most common:

Types of unit:

- Pixels (px)
- Percentages (%)
- Points (pt)

Let's look at how we can use percentages to change the height and width CSS properties of a `<div>`:

```html
<body>
  <div style="background-color: palegreen; height: 75%; width: 50%;">
    <p>The police remain baffled by the crime.</p>
    <p>There were no successful leads in the case.</p>
  </div>
</body>
```

percent value

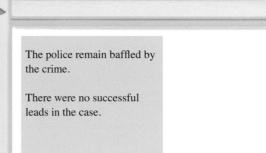

Did you notice?

When you calculate percentages, you are calculating what percentage of the screen you want your element to fill. If you change the size of your browser, the size of the element will also change.

The police remain baffled by the crime.

There were no successful leads in the case.

Pixels and points are used in exactly the same way as percentages. With these units, the size of your element will always stay the same, even if you change the size of your browser. Here, we've set the height and width CSS properties using values in pixels, and we've used the font-size CSS property to change the size of the text to a value in points.

pixel value   pixel value   point value

```html
<body>
  <div style="background-color: gold; height: 200px; width: 350px; font-size: 20pt;">
    <p>The Bond Brothers have never been caught.</p>
  </div>
</body>
```

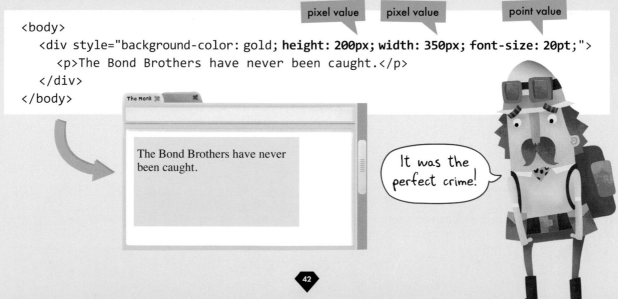

The Bond Brothers have never been caught.

It was the perfect crime!

creating Borders and Space with CSS

We can also use CSS properties to create borders and space around our HTML elements. To create a border around an HTML element, you have to use the border CSS property and set the values to the width, style, and color you want. Let's look at an example:

border property · width · style · color

```
<body>
    <div style="border: 4px solid green; width: 50%; height: 100px;">
        Professor Bairstone and Dr. Day are very excited by their discovery.
    </div>
</body>
```

We can also change how much space there is inside an HTML element by using the padding and margin CSS properties. You can set the values for the margin and padding at the top, bottom, left, and right of an HTML element. Let's take a look:

padding property · margin property

```
<body>
    <div style="padding: 25px; margin: 50px; border: 4px solid blue;
        width: 50%; height: 100px;">
        Ernest was also very happy with the find.<br/>
        Professor Bairstone gave him extra rations.
    </div>
</body>
```

Here, the padding CSS property creates 25px of space between the border of our `<div>` and the text about Ernest inside the `<div>`. The margin CSS property creates 50px of space between the border of our `<div>` and the edge of the page.

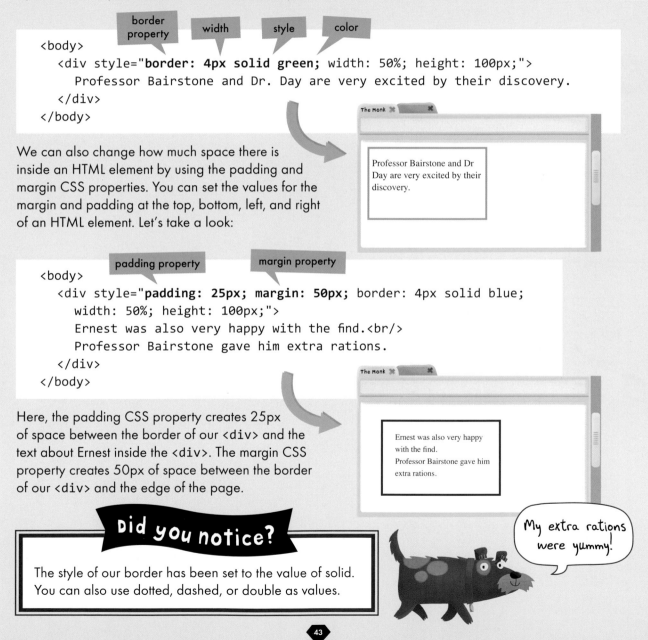

Did you notice?

The style of our border has been set to the value of solid. You can also use dotted, dashed, or double as values.

My extra rations were yummy!

CODE SKILLS ► USING MORE THAN ONE CSS PROPERTY

There are many different CSS properties you can use to make your web page for Professor Bairstone and Dr. Day look great. Now try using more than one CSS property in your code to change the page's layout and design.

1. Open up your text-editing program and create a new HTML file called **CSSproperties.html**. Copy and paste your code from **CSS.html** into your new file and modify it so that there are three `<div>` tags, like this:

```
<!DOCTYPE html>
<html>
<head>
   <title>The Monk Diamond</title>
</head>
<body>
   <div>
     Why was the diamond hidden in a cave?<br/>
     Who hid it there?
   </div>
   <div>
     Was it the Bond Brothers?<br/>
     Could they be watching the cave?
   </div>
   <div>
     Is the team safe?<br/>
     Their camp is very remote.
   </div>
</body>
</html>
```

I really hope we're not in danger!

We have to keep the diamond safe!

2. Change the color, font size, and position of the text in your first `<div>`. Use the color, font-size, and text-align CSS properties. Your code will look like this:

```
<div style="color: gray; font-size: 18pt; text-align: center;">
   Why was the diamond hidden in a cave?<br/>
   Who hid it there?
</div>
```

3. Change the width and height of your second `<div>` using the width and height CSS properties. Make your `<div>` 75% of the width of your page and 100px high. Add a background color and margin to your `<div>` too. Your code will look like this:

```
<div style="width: 75%; height: 100px; background-color: lightblue; margin: 20px;">
   Was it the Bond Brothers?<br/>
   Could they be watching the cave?
</div>
```

4. Let's try moving our third `<div>` to a different position on the page. Use the float CSS property to move your `<div>` to the right of your page. Also add a border and some padding to the `<div>` using the border and padding CSS properties. Your code will look like this:

```
<div style="float: right; border: 6px dotted red; padding: 20px;">
   Is the team safe?<br/>
   Their camp is very remote.
</div>
```

5. Save your HTML file and open it in your browser. Now try changing the values of all the CSS properties to ones of your choice and see what it does to your web page.

The Monk Di

Why was the diamond hidden in a cave?
Who hid it there?

Was it the Bond Brothers?
Could they be watching the cave?

Is the team safe?
Their camp is very remote.

USING CSS CLASSES

You might have noticed that adding lots of CSS properties to our HTML tags has made our lines of code long and difficult to read. It also takes time to type in the same CSS properties over and over again. To save time and make our code look neater, we now need to learn how to use CSS classes. CSS classes help you organize the CSS in the <body> of your page.

A CSS class is a very handy way of applying a group of CSS properties to any HTML element on your page. Programmers use CSS classes to keep their code as simple as possible. It's really important to do this when you are coding, as it means you are less likely to make mistakes. If, for example, you know that you want all the text in every <div> on your page to be a certain color and font size, rather than having to type the CSS properties into every <div>, you can use a CSS class to change all the <div> tags on your page at once.

Using the <head> Tag

So far we've mostly been coding inside the <body> of our page. It's now time to take a closer look at how we can use the <head>. Let's go back to the first page we built at the beginning of the mission:

```
<!DOCTYPE html>
<html>
<head>                          head tag
    <title>The Monk Diamond Discovery</title>
</head>
<body>
    <p>Professor Bairstone and Dr. Day have discovered the Monk Diamond.</p>
</body>
</html>
```

In every page we've built so far, the <title> tag has been nested inside the <head>. The content between the opening and closing <title> tags doesn't appear in the main <body> when we view it in our web browser.

We are going to add our CSS classes to our <head> tag. This is because the <head> is the best place to put information for our browser that we don't want to see drawn in the main <body> of the page.

The Monk

Professor Bairstone and Dr. Day have discovered the Monk Diamond.

46

The Style Tag: <style> and </style>

When you create a CSS class, you tell your browser that you are switching from HTML to CSS. You do this by using the <style> tag, which you nest inside the <head>. The <style> tag is just like all the other HTML tags you have used so far in this mission, except you put CSS inside it.

   Once you've opened the <style> tag, you can create a CSS class. Every CSS class needs a name. It's a good idea to make the name relate to the element you want to change. Let's look at how we can create a CSS class that changes the look of our text:

```
<head>
    <title>The Monk Diamond Discovery</title>
    <style>
    .text {
        text-align: center;
        font-size: 18pt;
        background-color: aqua;
    }
    </style>
</head>
```

style tag · CSS class name · dot · CSS properties · opening brace · closing brace

This is a different way of writing and structuring our code. CSS classes always start with the class name. It's up to you what you name your CSS classes, but before the class name there has to be a dot (.). Then there is a pair of braces ({ }). The braces tell your browser where the instructions it needs to follow begin and end. Inside the braces you put all the CSS properties you want to apply to the HTML element. As before, you separate the property from the value with a colon (:) and after the value put a semicolon (;).

   In this example, we have created a CSS class that we have named text. Every time we use this CSS class, we will change the text-align, font-size, and background-color CSS properties to the values we've selected.

Did you notice?

On your keyboard, the braces ({ }) keys are found to the right of the P key, on the same keys as the brackets. You need to press Shift to use them.

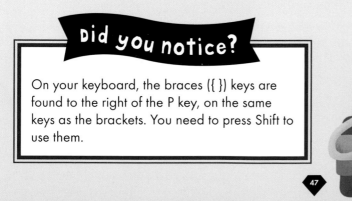

Turn the page to see how you make CSS classes work in the <body> of your code.

Using the class Attribute

Applying a CSS class to an HTML element in the <body> of our code is really simple. We just add the name we have chosen for our CSS class to the opening HTML tag for the element we want to change. Rather than using the style attribute, we now use the new class attribute. The class attribute is written and works in exactly the same way as all the other attributes we've used so far in this mission. Let's see what we have to do to apply our CSS class to HTML elements on our page:

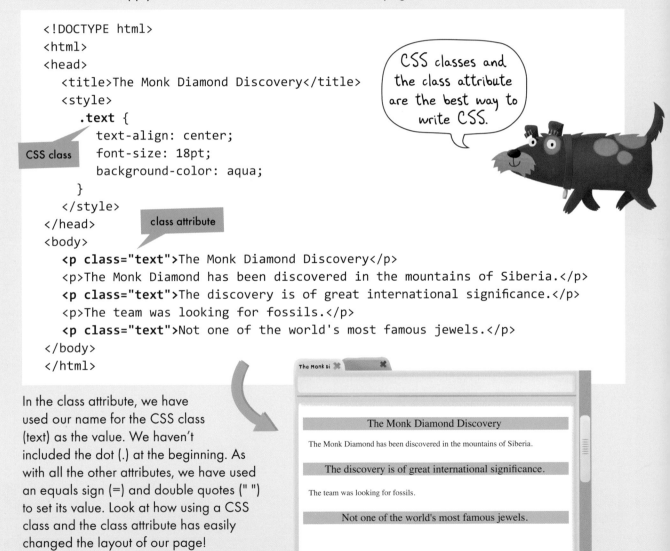

```
<!DOCTYPE html>
<html>
<head>
    <title>The Monk Diamond Discovery</title>
    <style>
      .text {
          text-align: center;
          font-size: 18pt;
          background-color: aqua;
      }
    </style>
</head>
<body>
    <p class="text">The Monk Diamond Discovery</p>
    <p>The Monk Diamond has been discovered in the mountains of Siberia.</p>
    <p class="text">The discovery is of great international significance.</p>
    <p>The team was looking for fossils.</p>
    <p class="text">Not one of the world's most famous jewels.</p>
</body>
</html>
```

CSS class

class attribute

> CSS classes and the class attribute are the best way to write CSS.

In the class attribute, we have used our name for the CSS class (text) as the value. We haven't included the dot (.) at the beginning. As with all the other attributes, we have used an equals sign (=) and double quotes (" ") to set its value. Look at how using a CSS class and the class attribute has easily changed the layout of our page!

The Monk Diamond Discovery

The Monk Diamond has been discovered in the mountains of Siberia.

The discovery is of great international significance.

The team was looking for fossils.

Not one of the world's most famous jewels.

code skills checklist ✔

CODING WITH CSS

- CSS is always made up of a property and a value. The property is the name of what you want to change, and the value is what you want to change it to. There are hundreds of different CSS properties and values.

- You separate the property from the value using a colon (:) and always use a semicolon (;) after the value. A hyphen (-) is used between words in CSS properties.

- Values can be given in words or numbers. Common units for numerical values include pixels (px), points (pt), and percentages (%).

- You can apply more than one CSS property to an HTML element. The best way to do this is to use a CSS class and the class attribute.

- You tell your browser you are switching from HTML to CSS by using the `<style>` tag. CSS classes are nested inside the `<head>` tag.

- When you choose a CSS class name, it needs to begin with a dot (.). The CSS properties and values you want to apply are put inside braces ({ }).

- You can apply a CSS class to any HTML element using the class attribute.

Here are some important things to remember when you write CSS!

Professor Bairstone is going to be so pleased with your web page!

CSS classes are a simple and effective way of using CSS to change your HTML elements. Let's try coding some CSS classes and using them with the class attribute to change the design of a web page.

1. Open up your text-editing program and create a new HTML file called **CSSclasses.html**. Copy and paste your code from **CSSproperties.html** into your new file and modify it so that the three `<div>` tags look like this:

Don't forget me! I was on the expedition too!

```
<!DOCTYPE html>
<html>
<head>
   <title>The Monk Diamond</title>
</head>
<body>
   <div>
     The Monk Diamond<br/>
     An incredible discovery
   </div>
   <br/>
   <div>
     Stolen diamond found on expedition in Siberia!
   </div>
   <br/>
   <div>
     Professor Bairstone and Dr. Day were looking for fossils in Siberia.<br/>
     They found the stolen diamond hidden inside a remote cave.
   </div>
</body>
</html>
```

1

2. Now add a `<style>` tag inside your `<head>`. Your code will look like this:

```
<head>
   <title>The Monk Diamond</title>
   <style>
   </style>
</head>
```

3. Between your opening and closing `<style>` tags, create a CSS class called header. Set the background-color, padding, text-align, and font-size CSS properties. Add the width and height CSS properties, too. Choose values for your properties. Your code will look like this:

```
<style>
   .header {
      background-color: blue;
      padding: 25px;
      text-align: center;
      font-size: 18pt;
      width: 100%;
      height: 25%;
   }
</style>
```

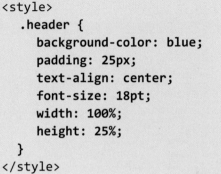

4. Apply your header CSS class to the first `<div>` in your `<body>` using the class attribute. Your code will look like this:

```
<div class="header">
   The Monk Diamond<br/>
   An incredible discovery
</div>
```

5. Create a second CSS class in your `<style>` tag and call it title. This new CSS class will come after your header CSS class. Set the font-size, text-align, and color properties. Choose values for your properties. Your code will look like this:

```
.title {
   font-size: 14pt;
   text-align: center;
   color: gray;
}
```

Why don't you try some different colors?

6. Apply your title CSS class to your second `<div>`. Your code will look like this:

```
<div class="title">
    Stolen diamond found on expedition in Siberia!
</div>
```

7. Create a third CSS class in your `<style>` tag and call it body. This CSS class will come after your title CSS class. Set the margin CSS property and value. Your code will look like this:

```
.body {
    margin: 20px;
}
```

8. Apply your body CSS class to your third `<div>`. Your code will look like this:

```
<div class="body">
    Professor Bairstone and Dr. Day were looking for fossils in Siberia.<br/>
    They found the stolen diamond hidden inside a remote cave.
</div>
```

9. Save your HTML file and open it in your browser. You will see that each CSS class changes the design of a `<div>`.

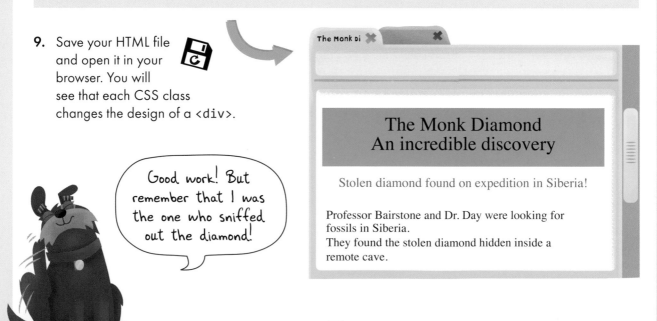

Good work! But remember that I was the one who sniffed out the diamond!

More Than One CSS class

If you want to make your CSS really effective, it's best to split your CSS classes into groups of CSS properties. This way, when you are designing and laying out a web page, you can apply more than one CSS class to your HTML element. It's really easy to use more than one CSS class at a time. All you have to do is add the names of the different classes to your class attribute. Let's take a look:

```html
<!DOCTYPE html>
<html>
<head>
    <title>The Monk Diamond</title>
    <style>
      .header {
          background-color: lightgreen;
          width: 70%;
          height: 50%;
      }
      .text {
          text-align: center;
          font-size: 18pt;
      }
      .padding {
          padding: 25px;
      }
    </style>
</head>
<body>
    <div class="header text padding">
        The Monk Diamond<br/>
        An incredible discovery
    </div>
</body>
</html>
```

The Monk Diamond
An incredible discovery

This is how we add more than one CSS class name to our class attribute.

Turn the page to find out more about the element selector.

Using CSS classes to Select HTML Elements

Another handy thing you can do with CSS classes is use them to change the CSS properties of a type of HTML element. To do this, you use something called the element selector. To use the element selector, you use the name of the element you want to change as the name of your CSS class. You shouldn't include the dot before the name of your CSS class. You also don't need to include a class attribute in the <body>.

So if you want all the text in your paragraphs to be centered and in a certain font size, you can create a CSS class called p, which will find and select your <p> tags. Let's take a look at what using the element selector does:

```
<!DOCTYPE html>
<html>
<head>
    <title>The Monk Diamond Discovery</title>
    <style>
      p {
          font-size: 16pt;
          text-align: center;
          background-color: lightblue;
      }
    </style>
</head>
<body>
    <p>The Monk Diamond was discovered by Professor Bairstone and Dr. Day.</p>
    <p>Ernest alerted them to its hiding place.</p>
    <p>It had been hidden in a crack in the rock.</p>
</body>
</html>
```

element selector

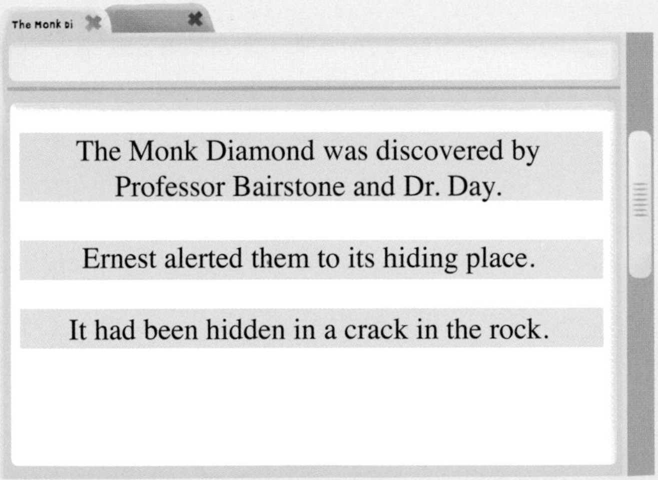

The Monk Di

The Monk Diamond was discovered by Professor Bairstone and Dr. Day.

Ernest alerted them to its hiding place.

It had been hidden in a crack in the rock.

Now, that's what I call clever coding!

The element selector has changed all our paragraphs without us having to add a class attribute to our <p> tags.

DO-IT-YOURSELF TASK
BUILD A WEB PAGE

In Mission 1, you learned lots of HTML and CSS Code Skills. Now it's time to use your new knowledge to build the web page for Professor Bairstone.

The Monk Diamond Discovery Web Page Brief

Build a web page about the discovery of the Monk Diamond. Use HTML and CSS to add text and images and create an interesting design. Include these things on your page:

- **A header banner**
- **A title banner**
- **Text about the Monk Diamond**
- **An image of the team**
- **An image of the diamond**
- **A Monk Diamond fact file**

Save your file in your **Coding** folder and call it **monkdiamonddiscovery.html**.

> Turn the page to see a code block for a finished web page.

> Don't forget to use the Get Coding! website if you get stuck.

This is what your web page would look like if you used this code!

```
<!DOCTYPE html>
<html>
<head>
    <title>The Monk Diamond</title>
    <style>
      body {
          margin: 0px;
      }
      .pad {
          padding: 25px;
      }
      .header {
          background-color: lightblue;
          color: black;
          height: 100px;
          font-size: 36pt;
          text-align: center;
      }
      .welcome {
          background-color: gray;
          color: white;
          font-size: 16pt;
          text-align: center;
          height: 40px;
          margin: 0px;
      }
      .main-text {
          width: 60%;
          float: left;
          background-color: beige;
      }
      .divs {
          margin: 5px;
          width: 25%;
          float: left;
          border: 4px solid lightblue;
      }
    </style>
```

```
</head>
 <body>
  <div class="header pad">
    The Monk Diamond Discovery
  </div>
  <div>
    <p class="welcome">
      Stolen Diamond Discovered in Siberia!
    </p>
  </div>
  <div class="main-text pad">
    <p>
      Professor Bairstone and Dr. Day have made a sensational discovery.<br/>
      They have discovered the Monk Diamond in a remote cave in Siberia.<br/>
      Professor Bairstone's dog, Ernest, sniffed out the diamond.
    </p>
    <p>
      The jewel was stolen three years ago from the House of Volkov.<br/>
      The prime suspects in the theft were the Bond Brothers.<br/>
      The team thinks the diamond had been hidden by the thieves.<br/>
      They sent this photo from their camp:
    </p>
    <img src="team.jpg" alt="The Team" style="height: 150px;"/>
  </div>
  <div class="divs pad">
    <img src="diamond.jpg" alt="Diamond" style="width: 150px;"/>
    <p style="text-align: center;">The Monk Diamond</p>
  </div>
  <div class="divs pad" style="text-align: center;">
    Fact File<br/>
    Carats: 300<br/>
    Color: Green<br/>
    Value: Over $10 million
  </div>
</body>
</html>
```

FUTURE CODE SKILLS

HTML and CSS are the most fundamental programming languages of the web. Now that you've mastered them, you can start building your own web pages. Knowing HTML and CSS is a great first step in a career in web design. Rather than using templates, you can create your own unique layouts — a fantastic skill. Mission accomplished!

Mission 2

CREATE A PASSWORD

- ◆ LEARN TO USE HYPERLINKS TO CONNECT WEB PAGES

- ◆ LEARN WHAT JAVASCRIPT IS AND HOW IT WORKS

- ◆ WRITE PROGRAMS IN JAVASCRIPT THAT RUN IN YOUR WEB BROWSER

- ◆ PROTECT A WEB PAGE BY USING JAVASCRIPT TO CREATE A PASSWORD

Dear Coder,

I'm Dr. Ruby Day, the scientist on the expedition with Professor Bairstone. We were hoping to discover dinosaur fossils. Instead we've found the stolen Monk Diamond!

I want to tell you about a strange event. Yesterday we were examining the cave where we found the diamond. I heard a rumbling noise, and Ernest started barking frantically. We looked up and saw a massive boulder rolling over the edge of the cliff above the cave! We jumped out of the way just in time, as the boulder landed exactly where we had been standing. In the commotion, Professor Bairstone tripped and sprained his ankle.

Professor Bairstone and I agree that the timing of the boulder falling is very suspicious. It seems too much of a coincidence for it to have happened just after we discovered a valuable stolen diamond. Professor Bairstone is convinced that the thieves have found out about our expedition and are trying to scare us off. He thinks the boulder is exactly the kind of dirty trick that the Bond Brothers, the main suspects in the Monk Diamond heist, would try.

We would leave the mountains now to take the diamond to safety, but unfortunately Professor Bairstone's sprained ankle means he can't make the treacherous descent just yet. While we are stuck in the mountains, I think the news about the discovery of the diamond needs to remain top secret. I am worried that the web page you built for Professor Bairstone could be accessed by the Bond Brothers and our safety compromised. Please could you add a password to the web page so that for now only Professor Bairstone and I can view the page? Use **Ernest300** as the password.

Thank you for all your help and hard work.

Very best wishes from the dangerous mountains,
Dr. Ruby Day

P.S. Prof. B. has asked me to send you this entry from the Explorer's Encyclopedia.

The Bond Brothers

From the Explorer's Encyclopedia: The Guide to Every Adventure

This entry is about the Bond Brothers. For more information about jewel robberies, see <u>Jewel Thefts</u>.

The **Bond Brothers** are a top-secret international gang of <u>jewel thieves</u>. According to <u>Interpol</u>, over the last fifteen years they have stolen <u>gems</u> worth a total of more than $500 million.

The gang's tactics are similar to those used by the famous gang the <u>Pink Panthers</u>.

**THE EXPLORER'S
ENCYCLOPEDIA**
The Guide to Every Adventure

Home page
Contents
Featured discoveries
Famous explorers
Historical expeditions

WANTED

FOR THE THEFT OF THE MONK DIAMOND
THE BOND BROTHERS

LIGHT FINGERS   **GEMMA THE GEM**   **TONY TWINKLES**

REWARD OF $1 MILLION

FOR INFORMATION LEADING TO THE RECOVERY OF THE MONK DIAMOND OR ARREST OF THE GANG

The Bond Brothers typically target exclusive jewelry stores all over the world. Their raids are exceptionally well planned, with the targets scoped out weeks in advance.

The Bond Brothers' tactics have included driving trucks through jewelry-store windows and drilling through store basements to access valuables kept in vaults. Members of the gang have disguised themselves as workers to confuse staff and then smashed open display cases.

Although the police were unable to prove it, most people think that the Bond Brothers are responsible for the unsolved theft of the Monk Diamond from the House of Volkov jewelry store in Moscow. Two members of the gang (a man and a woman) pretended to be looking for an engagement ring. While the woman distracted the staff, the man smashed open the Monk Diamond's display case with a pickax. The two then fled in a getaway car, which was posing as a taxi outside.

All the CCTV in and around the House of Volkov had been disabled for the hour in which the crime took place. Interpol therefore believes that one of the gang is also skilled in cybercrime.

USING HYPERLINKS

In the Mission Brief, Dr. Day asked you to create a password. The password will keep the Bond Brothers from finding out about the discovery of the Monk Diamond. In this mission, you are going to learn how to make the password.

We have to use a new programming language called JavaScript to make the password. But before we can get started on coding the password, you first need to learn how to use HTML to link two web pages. We need to be able to link the web page that asks the user to enter the password to the web page you built for Professor Bairstone.

Hyperlinks (or links, as they are normally known) are found on most web pages and are essential for creating the groups of web pages we call websites. A hyperlink can be a word, number, phrase, or image that you click on. When you click on the link, your web browser takes you to either a different place in your current web page or a completely new web page.

The Anchor Tag: <a> and </a>

Hyperlinks are made using an HTML tag called the anchor <a> tag. The opening tag is <a> and the closing tag is </a>. Inside the opening <a> tag you have to include an href attribute. The href attribute contains the URL (or web address) your browser needs to link to the new web page. Let's take a look:

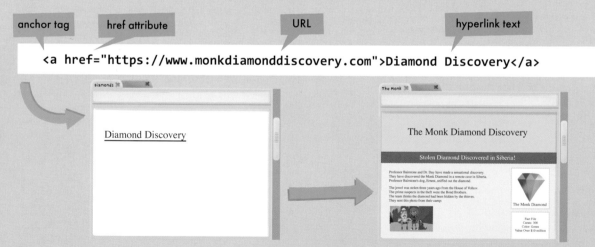

```
anchor tag    href attribute         URL                    hyperlink text
<a href="https://www.monkdiamonddiscovery.com">Diamond Discovery</a>
```

We've set the value of our href attribute to the URL for the Monk Diamond Discovery page. We've done this in exactly the same way as we set the values of all the attributes in Mission 1: by using the equals sign (=) and double quotes (" ") to enclose the URL. The text between the opening and closing <a> tags becomes your link. When you click on this text, you will be taken to the Monk Diamond page.

CODE SKILLS ► CREATING A HYPERLINK

Creating hyperlinks is an important skill to master when building websites, as they let the user easily access pieces of content. Let's create a web page with a hyperlink.

1. Open up your text-editing program. Create a new HTML file called **links.html**. Type this code into your new file:

```
<!DOCTYPE html>
<html>
<head>
    <title>Links</title>
</head>
<body>
</body>
</html>
```

2. Let's make our hyperlink. Add an anchor `<a>` tag with an empty href attribute to the `<body>` of your page. Your code will look like this:

```
<body>
    <a href=" "></a>
</body>
```

3. Choose a word or phrase to be the text for your hyperlink on your web page. Put it between your opening and closing `<a>` tags. Your code will look like this:

```
<body>
    <a href=" ">Click here</a>
</body>
```

4. Now choose the URL you want your hyperlink to connect to. Set it as the value of your href attribute. Your code will look like this:

```
<body>
    <a href="https://www.google.com">
        Click here</a>
</body>
```

5. Save your HTML file and open it in your web browser. You will see the text between your `<a>` tags displayed on-screen. When you click the hyperlink text, your web browser will link to your URL.

Try clicking your new link!

Linking Web Pages

To protect the information about the Monk Diamond, we first need to make a new web page. This new web page will be the first page that the user sees. If the user gets the password correct, they will be sent to the Monk Diamond web page. If they get the password wrong, nothing will happen. By linking our pages, we create a website.

We need to use a hyperlink to connect our two pages. If your web pages are saved in the same place on your computer, you don't need to provide your web browser with the URL — you can just use the file name as the URL. So if we make sure we have both HTML files saved in our **Coding** folder, we can use code like this:

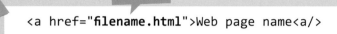

file name

```
<a href="filename.html">Web page name<a/>
```

When we create our new password web page and save the HTML file in our **Coding** folder, we can link the new web page to the web page we built for Professor Bairstone in Mission 1 really easily. All we need to do is use the <a> tag and href attribute on each of our pages, like this:

Page 2: monkdiamonddiscovery.html

```
<!DOCTYPE html>
<html>
<head>
  <title>The Monk Diamond</title>
</head>
<body>
  <a href="password.html">
    Click here to log out</a>
</body>
</html>
```

file name

Page 1: password.html

```
<!DOCTYPE html>
<html>
<head>
  <title>Password</title>
</head>
<body>
  <a href="monkdiamonddiscovery.html">
    Click here to visit the Monk
    Diamond web page</a>
</body>
</html>
```

file name

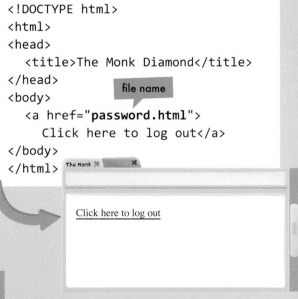

Clicking on the link in our password page takes us to our Monk Diamond web page. And clicking on the link in the Monk Diamond page takes us back to our password page.

CODE SKILLS ► LINKING WEB PAGES

Let's learn how to use hyperlinks to link two web pages and build
a very simple website.

1. Open up your text-editing program. Create a
new HTML file called **page1.html**. Make sure
it is saved in your **Coding** folder. Type this code
into your new file:

```
<!DOCTYPE html>
<html>
<head>
   <title>Page 1</title>
</head>
<body>
</body>
</html>
```

2. Create a second HTML file called **page2.html**.
Make sure it is saved in your **Coding** folder.
Then copy and paste your code from **page1.html**
into your new file. Modify the code so that it
looks like this:

```
<!DOCTYPE html>
<html>
<head>
   <title>Page 2</title>
</head>
<body>
</body>
</html>
```

3. Now create a hyperlink that connects your first
page to your second page. On your first page,
add the <a> tag with an href attribute. Set the value
of the href to the file name of your second page.
Then add some text between the opening and
closing <a> tags to make your hyperlink, like this:

```
<body>
   <a href="page2.html">Page 2</a>
</body>
```

4. Now open your second page. Create a
hyperlink that takes you back to your first page.
Your code will look like this:

```
<body>
   <a href="page1.html">Back to Page 1</a>
</body>
```

 Save your files and open them in your
browser. You will be able to link the two
pages.

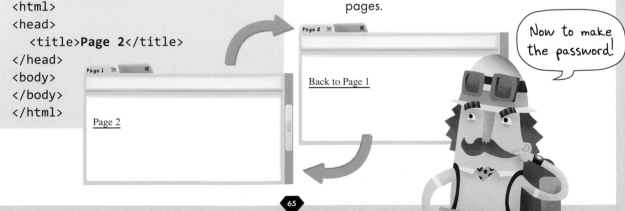

Now to make
the password!

CODING WITH JAVASCRIPT

Hyperlinks are an important first step in creating a web page that responds to the user. But if we want to code a page that is really interactive and changes according to what the user does, we need to use a new programming language called JavaScript with our HTML.

JavaScript is the most popular programming language in the world. It transforms an HTML and CSS web page by making it interactive. We need JavaScript to do all sorts of useful things, such as making buttons and alerts and storing information. In this mission, we are going to learn how we can use JavaScript with HTML to create a password, so that the information about the Monk Diamond is kept safe from the cybercriminal in the Bond Brothers gang.

We saw in Mission 1 how HTML documents are made up of different elements and that you use attributes to change those elements. JavaScript also has its own syntax, or set of rules, for writing code. JavaScript syntax is made up of pieces of code called statements, variables, operators, and functions. Let's learn about them and see how we can use them to build the password.

Adding JavaScript to Your HTML Page

Before you can start writing JavaScript, you need to tell your browser that you are switching from HTML to JavaScript. You do this by using the `<script>` tag. If you don't put your JavaScript code between the opening and closing `<script>` tags, your code won't run. You can have as many `<script>` tags as you want in your HTML document, and you can put them inside either the `<head>` or `<body>` on your page.

```
<!DOCTYPE html>
<html>
<head>
    <title>Password</title>
</head>
<body>
    <script>           ◄— script tag
    </script>
</body>
</html>
```

Here, the `<script>` tag is inside the `<body>` of our page. Sometimes we call this a `<script>` block.

2

Statements

When we write an instruction for our browser in JavaScript, we call this writing a statement. JavaScript programs normally contain many statements. A statement usually starts with a keyword that tells you what action it will perform. It always ends with a semicolon (;). Your browser runs one statement after another in the order they are written. Let's look at some JavaScript statements. When we save this code and run it in our browser, this happens:

```
<!DOCTYPE html>
<html>
<head>
    <title>Password</title>
</head>
<body>
    <script>
        alert("We need a password urgently!");
        alert("Use the password Ernest300");
    </script>
</body>
</html>
```

semicolon

statements

We need a password urgently!

OK

Use the password Ernest300

OK

The two statements between the opening and closing `<script>` tags have run one after another, popping up two alert boxes with different messages inside. An alert is a piece of JavaScript called a function, and it's built in to your web browser. We'll learn more about it later in the mission.

JavaScript is case sensitive, so it's important to make sure you have used the correct capital letters. When you choose a name for a piece of JavaScript, you can't leave spaces between words. A good way to write two words is to use **camelCase**.

CODE WORDS

CAMELCASE is the practice of joining two words to form one word. The first word starts with a lowercase letter and the second word begins with an uppercase letter, but there is no space between them, like the hump of a camel. An example of camelCase is sayHello.

VARIABLES

These are important!

Variables are an important part of JavaScript. They are a way to store information in your web browser for a short period of time. You can then use the stored data to build programs that make your web page interactive. Without variables, your browser has no way of remembering information.

So when we use JavaScript to code a program that will check a password, we need to use a variable to store the data for the correct password. Without a variable, our browser won't be able to check whether the user has entered a correct password.

Variables store data in the form of words or numbers. You have to code variables in a certain way. You always have to tell your browser you are creating a variable. This is called defining a variable. Let's look at how we create a variable that will store Ernest's name:

Ernest is a very good name!

```
var dogName = "Ernest";
```

variable keyword | variable name | value

Variables are always written in the same way. Every piece of JavaScript tells your browser a different piece of information and will be important when you build a program.

A variable needs:

- **A keyword**
  To define a variable, you have to use the variable (var) keyword. It tells your browser that you are creating a variable.

- **A variable name**
  The next part of a variable is the variable name. You can give your variable any name you like. The only rule with variable names is that they can't have spaces (so use camelCase instead) and can't begin with a number.

- **A value**
  You then have to give your variable a value using the equals sign (=). Doing this is called assigning a value. If the value of your variable is text, you have to put the value in double quotes (" "). You can include spaces in your values. After the value, you have to include a semicolon (;).

Operators

Operators are another key part of JavaScript. They are a way of changing the value of a variable. Different kinds of operators do different things to the information in your variable.

Assignment Operators

Can you spot the use of camelCase?

Assignment operators allow you to create and set the values of your variables.

Equals (=): You use the equals sign (=) to give your variable a value. You can use it to set variables to both numbers and words. If your variable is a number, it doesn't have to be in double quotes (" "). Here's an example where the value is set to a number:

```
var teamMembers = 3;
```
assignment operator

And here's an example where the value is set to words and needs double quotes (" "):

```
var expeditionLeader = "Professor Bairstone";
```

Arithmetic Operators

Arithmetic operators are a way of using math calculations to change the values of your variables. They are a useful way of creating a numerical value for a variable.

Addition (+): You use the addition operator (+) to add numbers to create a value. Here, the value of our campRations variable will be set to 3.

```
var campRations = 2 + 1;
```
addition operator

subtraction operator

Subtraction (−): You use the subtraction operator (−) to subtract numbers to create a value. Here, the value of our dogBiscuits variable will be set to 1.

```
var dogBiscuits = 5 - 4;
```

Always make sure you use a semicolon at the end of the variable.

Don't forget to put text values in double quotes.

CODE SKILLS ► USING VARIABLES AND OPERATORS

Variables and operators are important parts of the JavaScript programming language. Let's code some simple JavaScript programs using them.

1. Before we can write any JavaScript, we need to create an HTML file with a `<script>` tag in the `<body>`. Open up your text-editing program. Create a new HTML file called **variables.html**. Type this code into your new file:

```html
<!DOCTYPE html>
<html>
<head>
   <title>Variables</title>
</head>
<body>
   <script>
   </script>
</body>
</html>
```

2. Now try writing some JavaScript. Create a variable between the opening and closing `<script>` tags. Give your variable a name and then use the assignment operator (=) to set the value of your variable. Let's try with a number, like this:

```html
<script>
   var diamondCarats = 300;
</script>
```

Don't forget that JavaScript is case sensitive, so make sure you keep the cases the same in your code block. Also remember the semicolon (;) at the end. If you save your HTML file and open it in your browser, nothing will happen — but don't worry. You have stored 300 in your diamondCarats variable.

3. Let's use the alert function to make sure your variable has been stored in your browser. Underneath your variable, type this code:

```html
<script>
   var diamondCarats = 300;
   alert(diamondCarats);
</script>
```

What we're doing is asking our browser to run the built-in alert function. Whatever value is in our diamondCarats variable will be displayed in an alert.

> Check to make sure pop-ups haven't been disabled in your browser. Search online for how to disable the pop-up blocker in the browser you are using.

Save your HTML file and refresh your page. An alert will pop up and you will see the value of your diamondCarats variable displayed on-screen. Click OK and your alert will vanish. Refresh your page and the alert will reload.

4. Now let's code a new variable, using the addition operator (+), to find the total number of people and dogs in Professor Bairstone's team. Let's call our variable teamMembers and set an alert to show the value of our variable. Modify the `<script>` block so that it looks like this:

```
<script>
   var teamMembers = 2 + 1;
   alert(teamMembers);
</script>
```

Save your file and refresh your page. Your alert will be the value of your teamMembers variable. Click OK.

5. Finally, let's try creating a variable using the assignment operator (=) to store text in our variable. Don't forget that you need double quote marks (" ") around the text. Set an alert to show the value of your variable. Modify the code in your file so that it looks like this:

```
<script>
   var jewelThieves = "The Bond Brothers";
   alert(jewelThieves);
</script>
```

When you save your file and refresh your page, you will see your text displayed in an alert.

Well done! You've just written your first JavaScript programs!

COMPARISON OPERATORS

In addition to assigning values or performing calculations, operators can be used to compare the values of variables. Being able to compare values allows us to make our web pages more interactive. Using comparison operators, we can write code that does different things depending on the values of our variables. Here are some of the different comparison operators you can use:

These operators can be used in JavaScript statements to ask questions about our variables. Then we can write code that makes different things happen depending on the answer to the question. Instructions for our browser that use comparison operators are called if statements and else statements. These types of statements are called conditional statements, because they depend on the value, or condition, of the variable.

Operator	Meaning
==	Equal to
!=	Not equal to
>	Greater than
<	Less than
>=	Greater than or equal to
<=	Less than or equal to

IF STATEMENTS

If statements are a way of telling our browser to perform an instruction only if the condition of our variable is true. If the condition of our variable is false, our browser won't perform the instruction in the code.

We have to structure if statements in a certain way. We start them with the statement keyword (if). Then we open a pair of parentheses and put the rule for our if statement inside them. Then we open a pair of braces ({ }). Inside them we put the instruction we want to happen only when our if statement is true.

Let's look at an example where we've used the equal to operator (==) to create an if statement. Here, the value of our variable is set to Dr. Day using the assignment operator (=). We then create an if statement by asking our browser to check if the value in our variable is equal to (==) Dr. Day. Then we ask our browser to pop up an alert if our condition is true.

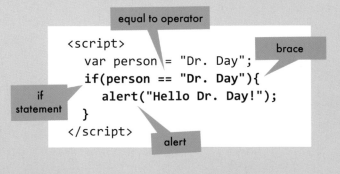

equal to operator

brace

if statement

alert

```
<script>
    var person = "Dr. Day";
    if(person == "Dr. Day"){
        alert("Hello Dr. Day!");
    }
</script>
```

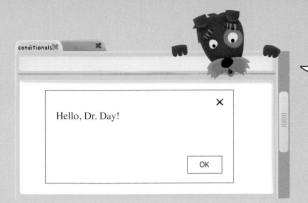

We've used an if statement to code a program that will say hello to Dr. Day!

Now, if we change the value of our variable to a value that isn't equal to Dr. Day, nothing will happen. This is because the if statement is false. Our browser won't run the code inside the braces, and no alert will pop up.

```
<script>
  var person = "Ernest";
  if(person == "Dr. Day") {
    alert("Hello, Dr. Day!");
  }
</script>
```

You can use the other comparison operators in that table to check all sorts of different things. You can see if things are not equal (!=), or you can use the greater than (>) and less than (<) operators to check if a number is bigger or smaller than another number. Let's look at using the greater than operator (>) to create an if statement.

greater than operator

```
<script>
  var diamondCarats = 300;
  if(diamondCarats > 299) {
    alert("Valuable Diamond Alert!");
  }
</script>
```

Here, the value of our variable is set to 300. We create an if statement by asking our browser to check whether the value in our variable is greater than (>) 299. Then we ask our browser to pop up an alert if our condition is true. The Monk Diamond is 300 carats, so the alert will pop up.

Notice how the closing brace lines up with the keyword.

Using if statements in your JavaScript code means you can build more complex programs that change according to the value in a variable. Let's build a program that uses an if statement.

1. Open up your text-editing program. Create a new HTML file called **ifstatements.html**. Type this code into your new file:

```
<!DOCTYPE html>
<html>
<head>
  <title>Conditionals</title>
</head>
<body>
  <script>
  </script>
</body>
```

2. Create an if statement using the equal to operator (==). Make an alert pop up if the condition of a variable is true. First, create a variable called dogName between your `<script>` tags. Then create your if statement and alert. Don't forget to put the instruction for the if statement in parentheses and the instruction for your alert in braces ({ }). Your code will look like this:

```
<script>
  var dogName = "Ernest";
  if(dogName == "Ernest") {
     alert("You discovered the Monk Diamond!");
  }
</script>
```

3. Save your HTML file and open it in your browser. An alert will pop up.

conditionals

You discovered the Monk Diamond! ×

OK

I certainly did discover that diamond! It wasn't such a clever hiding place after all.

4. In the value of your variable, try changing Ernest to your own name, so the condition of the if statement is false. Save your file and refresh your page. The alert will not pop up.

ELSE STATEMENTS

Else statements are used with if statements to make web pages even more interactive. You use an else statement after an if statement to change which block of code is run by your browser. If the condition of your if statement is false, your browser will run the alternative else statement.

Else statements are written in exactly the same way as if statements — you just have to use the else keyword instead. You put the code you want to run inside braces ({ }). Let's take a look at an example of an if statement and an else statement working together:

```
<script>
  var name = "Tony Twinkles";
  if(name == "Dr. Day") {
    alert("Access Granted!");
  }
  else {
    alert("Access Denied!");
  }
</script>
```

else statement

If we run this code in our browser, an alert will pop up. The value in our variable is the name of one of the Bond Brothers and not equal to (==) Dr. Day. Because the condition of the if statement was false, our browser ran the else statement. But if the value of our variable had been equal to (==) Dr. Day and the condition of our if statement had been true, the else statement would not have run. The if statement would have run instead, and the "Access Granted" alert would have popped up.

conditionals

Access Denied!

OK

That's a clever way to stop the Bond Brothers!

Hmph! How am I going to find out if they have the jewel?

CODE SKILLS ► CODING ELSE STATEMENTS

Now we should learn how to use an else statement with an if statement in a block of JavaScript code. Let's try coding a program that uses both types of conditional statement.

1. Open up your text-editing program. Create a new HTML file called **elsestatements.html**. Then copy and paste your code from **ifstatements.html** into your new file. Modify the code so that it looks like this:

```
<!DOCTYPE html>
<html>
<head>
   <title>Conditionals</title>
</head>
<body>
   <script>
   </script>
</body>
```

2. Create a new if statement in your `<script>` block using the less than or equal to operator (<=). Make the condition of your if statement false. Your code will look like this:

```
<script>
   var diamondValue = 10;
   if(diamondValue <= 9.9) {
      alert("Value: Under $10 million!");
   }
</script>
```

3. Now add an else statement after your if statement. This statement will run if the condition of the if statement is false. Your code will look like this:

```
<script>
   var diamondValue = 10;
   if(diamondValue <= 9.9) {
      alert("Value: Under $10 million!");
   }
   else {
      alert("Value: Over $10 million!");
   }
</script>
```

4. Save your HTML file and open it in your browser. Your else statement will run and an alert will pop up.

code skills checklist ✔

WRITING JAVASCRIPT

- JavaScript always has to be written inside the `<script>` tag, so that your browser knows you are switching from HTML to a new programming language. You can put `<script>` tags in the `<head>` or `<body>` of your page.

- Just like HTML and CSS, JavaScript is written in a special way and has its own syntax. It is a case-sensitive language. You should leave spaces between pieces of code to make them easier to read.

- Each instruction you give your browser in JavaScript is called a statement. Statements have to end in a semicolon (;). Braces ({ }) are used to group statements into a block of code to be run all at once by your browser.

- Statements normally start with a keyword that tells you the action the statement will perform.

- You can store information in your browser using variables. Variables have a name and a value, which can be either text or numbers. If the value is text, it has to be in double quotes (" "). If your variable name has two words, write it using camelCase.

- To change or set the values of your variables, you can use assignment operators, arithmetic operators, and comparison operators.

- If statements and else statements are known as conditional statements. Using conditional statements allows us to make our code do different things depending on the value of a variable.

> Using JavaScript helps us make interactive web pages that respond to the user.

FUNCTIONS

Another important part of JavaScript coding is learning how to create and use functions. You create a function by grouping JavaScript statements. The statements grouped in the function work together to perform a particular action. The function won't run until you tell your browser to run it. This is known as calling a function. Let's take a look at how you create a function that will pop up an alert and then call it:

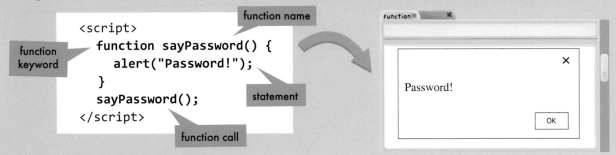

```
<script>
  function sayPassword() {
    alert("Password!");
  }
  sayPassword();
</script>
```

function keyword

function name

statement

function call

Functions always have to be written in the same way. Each part is an important instruction for your browser.

A function needs:

- **The function keyword**
  To define and create a function, use the function keyword.

- **A function name**
  Then give your function a name. The name should be short and explain the action the function performs. The name always ends with a pair of parentheses.

- **Braces**
  After the function name, open a pair of braces ({ }). All the statements you want grouped in the function go inside the braces.

- **Statements**
  Statements form the body of your function. You can use as many statements as you want, and the block of code will run in your browser whenever you call the function.

- **A function call**
  To call our function and run the block of code, you have to type the name of the function (including the parentheses) followed by a semicolon. After you have defined your function, you can call your function anywhere in your `<script>` block.

Built-in Functions

In addition to grouping statements to create your own functions, you can also use functions that are built in to your browser. A built-in function is an action your browser knows how to perform without your having to write any code. A programmer has already done the hard work for you. All you have to do is give your browser the name of the built-in function and the information it needs to run.

JavaScript has many built-in functions. You've already been using one in this mission: the alert function. To use the alert function, all you do is type "alert" and your browser pops up the alert box. Built-in functions save you time and let you do more complex things when you are programming.

Functions and Arguments

To make a function perform a task, you sometimes have to give it a piece of information so it can run. When we put information inside a function, we say that we have passed our function an argument. You have been passing an argument to a function every time you have used the alert function. Let's take a look at what an argument looks like:

argument

function

```
alert("Access Denied!");
```

The information in parentheses after the name of the function is our argument. Our browser needs the argument to know what text to display in the alert box. Without the argument, the alert function wouldn't work properly.

Arguments can be in the form of text, numbers, or variables. If you are passing your function a piece of text to use as an argument, it needs to be in double quotes (" "). If you are passing it the name of a variable, you just use the variable name without quotes, like this:

```
var bondBrothers = "Dangerous jewel thieves!";
alert(bondBrothers);
```

variable passed as argument

You can pass arguments to any kind of function. You might have wondered why function names and function calls always end with a pair of parentheses. It's so you can pass the function an argument. Turn the page to see how to do it.

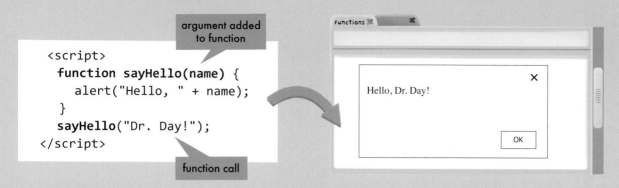

```
<script>
  function sayHello(name) {
    alert("Hello, " + name);
  }
  sayHello("Dr. Day!");
</script>
```

argument added to function

function call

Hello, Dr. Day!

OK

In this piece of code, we have created a function that will pop up an alert. We do this by adding an argument to our function. This kind of argument is called a parameter. We then code an alert that tells our browser to pop up some text plus the argument. We then tell the browser the name to insert in the alert by putting it in the function call.

The return statement

So far we have been giving our functions pieces of information in arguments. We can also make our functions give us pieces of information back as values. When a function gives back a piece of information, we say it has returned the information. To make a function return a piece of information, we have to use a return statement inside the function. The value in the return statement can be text, numbers, or a variable, and it becomes the value of the function. Let's take a look at how we can use a return statement to give us a piece of text:

function name

return statement

value to return

```
<script>
  function getName() {
    return "Dr. Day";
  }
  var scientist = getName();
  alert(scientist);
</script>
```

Dr. Day

OK

> Functions will often perform an action and return the result to the rest of your code.

In this example, we've created a function called getName. We want our function to give us Dr. Day's name as a value, so we've used a return statement and set her name as the value. We've then stored the function name as the variable value. When the alert pops up, it will pop up with the value of the return.

CODE SKILLS ► FUNCTIONS AND ARGUMENTS

Let's try grouping statements and creating a function. We should also try out the return statement, because it will be very useful when we create our password for Dr. Day.

1. Open up your text-editing program. Create a new HTML file called **functions.html**. Type this code into your new file:

```
<!DOCTYPE html>
<html>
<head>
    <title>Functions</title>
</head>
<body>
    <script>
    </script>
</body>
</html>
```

2. Inside your <script> block, create a function called checkAccess that will pop up an alert when you call it. Your code will look like this:

```
<script>
    function checkAccess() {
        alert("Restricted access!");
    }
    checkAccess();
</script>
```

3. Save your HTML file and open it in your browser. An alert will pop up.

Functio

×
Restricted access!

OK

4. Now change your checkAccess function so that it contains a return statement. Store the name of your function in a variable. Then make an alert pop up to show the value of your variable:

```
<script>
    function checkAccess() {
        return "Expedition team only!";
    }
    var webPage = checkAccess();
    alert(webPage);
</script>
```

Functio

×
Expedition team only!

OK

Save and refresh your page. A new alert will pop up.

MAKING JAVASCRIPT WORK WITH HTML

We've seen throughout this mission how you can add JavaScript to your HTML web page by writing it inside the `<script>` tag. But now we need to learn how to make our JavaScript code run when the user clicks on an HTML element. If we want something to happen when the user clicks on a piece of text or an image on our page, we have to add JavaScript to our HTML tags. Luckily there's an attribute that lets us do this.

Attributes! You know all about them from Mission 1.

The onclick Attribute

It's really easy to make a piece of JavaScript run when the user clicks on an HTML element on your page. All you need to do is include the onclick attribute (or the "onclick") in the HTML tag you want to make interactive. Then when the user clicks on the HTML element in their browser, the JavaScript code will run.

The onclick attribute is just like all the other attributes we've used in the missions so far. You add the attribute to the opening tag of the HTML element you want the user to click on. You then set the value of the onclick to the piece of JavaScript you want to run, using the equals sign (=) and double quotes (" "). Don't forget the semicolon (;). You can put any JavaScript you want inside an onclick. Let's take a look:

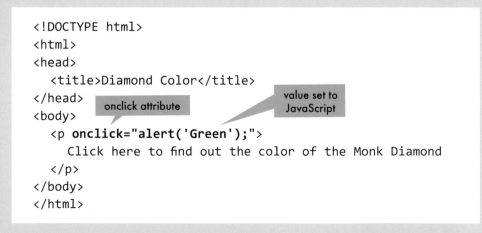

```
<!DOCTYPE html>
<html>
<head>
   <title>Diamond Color</title>
</head>
<body>
   <p onclick="alert('Green');">
      Click here to find out the color of the Monk Diamond
   </p>
</body>
</html>
```

onclick attribute

value set to JavaScript

2

When the user clicks on the text between the opening and closing <p> tags, the JavaScript function in our onclick runs. An alert will pop up.

Did you know that green diamonds are extremely rare?

Diamond co

Click

Green

×

OK

Did you notice?

We used single quotes (' ') around the argument we passed to our alert function. This is because we had already used double quotes to set the value of the onclick attribute. Always use single quotes inside double quotes, or your code won't run.

Using true and false with the Return Statement

You can also use your onclick attribute to stop your browser from following an instruction in a piece of code. To do this you use a return statement in your onclick, and set its value to "false".

Return is a **reserved word** in JavaScript. If you use a return statement and set it to the value "true", your browser will keep running the code. But if you use "false" as a value in your return statement, your browser will stop running the code immediately.

I'm worried those pesky Bond Brothers might be around— please hurry with the password!

CODE WORDS

RESERVED WORDS are words that cannot be used as function or variable names. This is because they are special commands that your browser understands. You don't need to put reserved words in double quotes (" ").

The onclick Attribute and Hyperlinks

We can create a very useful piece of JavaScript with the onclick attribute and the value "false". You can use the onclick and the return statement to stop a hyperlink from working when a user clicks on it. This will be very useful when we code our password later in the mission. If the user gets the password wrong, they won't be taken to the Monk Diamond web page.

To do this, you first create your hyperlink exactly the same way we did at the start of the mission, using the anchor <a> tag and the href attribute, like this:

```
<body>
  <a href="monkdiamonddiscovery.html">
     Click here to visit the Monk Diamond web page
  </a>
</body>
```

Then you add the onclick attribute and the return statement. Set the value of the return statement to "false", like this:

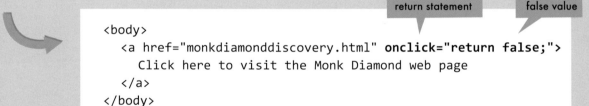

return statement   false value

```
<body>
  <a href="monkdiamonddiscovery.html" onclick="return false;">
     Click here to visit the Monk Diamond web page
  </a>
</body>
```

Using "false" as the value of our onclick means that nothing will happen when the user clicks on the link.

This will help keep our web page hidden!

CODE SKILLS ► MAKING HTML CODE RUN JAVASCRIPT

Practice using the HTML onclick attribute to run a piece of JavaScript code. Knowing how to do this will mean you can make HTML elements respond to the user.

1. Open up your text-editing program. Create a new HTML file called **onclick.html**. Type this code into your new file:

```
<!DOCTYPE html>
<html>
<head>
    <title>Onclick</title>
</head>
<body>
</body>
</html>
```

2. In your <body> create a hyperlink that will take your user to Google. Use the anchor <a> tag and href attribute. Set the value to the Google URL. Your code will look like this.

```
<body>
    <a href="https://www.google.com">
    Google
    </a>
</body>
```

3. Now add your onclick attribute to your opening <a> tag. Set the value of your onclick to a JavaScript alert. Remember to use single quotes (' ') for the alert argument. Your code will look like this:

```
<a href="https://www.google.com" onclick="alert('Redirecting to Google');">
    Google
</a>
```

4. Save your HTML file and open it in your browser. When you click on the link, an alert will pop up. When you click OK, you will be taken to Google.

5. Now stop your hyperlink from taking you to Google. Use a return statement in your onclick like this:

```
<a href="https://www.google.com" onclick="return false;">
    Google
</a>
```

 Save your file and refresh your page. When you click on the link, your page won't connect to Google.

CREATING YOUR PASSWORD PAGE

Now that you know how to use the onclick attribute to make your HTML elements interactive, we can start building our password web page for Dr. Day.
Let's start with the basic HTML structure of our page:

```
<!DOCTYPE html>
<html>
<head>
  <title>Password</title>
<style>
  body {
    background-color: lightblue;
    padding: 30px;
  }
</style>
</head>
<body>
  <p style="font-size: 30pt;">THE MONK DIAMOND DISCOVERY</p>
  <p>Please enter the password to view this website.</p>
  <p>Password:</p>
  <a href="monkdiamonddiscovery.html">
    Click here to submit password and view website
  </a>
</body>
</html>
```

CSS class

Don't forget: the top-secret password is **Ernest300**.

hyperlink

Here, we've created a simple web page using HTML and CSS. We've included a hyperlink that links to our Monk Diamond Discovery web page. But there isn't anywhere on our page where the user can enter their password. We need to create a box so that the user can type it in.

Password ✖   ✖

THE MONK DIAMOND DISCOVERY

Please enter the password to view this website.

Password:

Click here to submit password and view website

86

The input Tag: `<input/>`

Websites often need you to type in information. It's how you log in to an online account, buy movie tickets, or use a search engine. So asking your user to type in information is a common part of coding. It's called asking for user input.

There are lots of tags you can use to ask for user input, but the one you will use the most is the `<input/>` tag. It's great for creating boxes on your page so your user can enter data. It's a self-closing tag, and you include two attributes inside it: the id attribute and the type attribute. As you already know, you set the value of these attributes using the equals sign (=) and double quotes (" "). Let's take a look at how we would use the `<input/>` tag on our page:

```
<body>
   <p style="font-size: 30pt;">THE MONK DIAMOND DISCOVERY</p>
   <p>Please enter the password to view this website.</p>
   <p>Password:<input id="passwordBox" type="text"/></p>
   <a href="monkdiamonddiscovery.html">
     Click here to submit password and view website
   </a>
</body>
```

type attribute

id attribute

Using the `<input/>` tag with these two attributes creates a box that we can type our password into.

You use the id attribute to give your `<input/>` tag a unique name. You have to choose the name of your id attribute. Make sure it's easy to remember. Here, we've set the value of the id attribute to "passwordBox".

Doing this allows us to use the value inside the `<input/>` tag in our JavaScript. We use the id attribute to tell our browser exactly which piece of data we want it to use. Without the id attribute, your browser will not be able to find the password and check whether the password is correct.

Password

THE MONK DIAMOND DISCOVERY

Please enter the password to view this website.

Password: Ernest300

Click here to submit password and view website

Look, you can enter the password!

The type Attribute

There are lots of different kinds of <input/> tags, so you need to use the type attribute to tell your browser exactly what sort of <input/> tag you need. You have to choose from defined values for your type attribute. Here are some of the common type attributes you can use inside your <input/> tag:

Attribute value	What does it do?
text	Creates a box for entering text
password	Creates a box for entering a password
button	Creates a clickable button (with JavaScript)
checkbox	Creates a box the user can tick or untick

You may have noticed on the previous page that when we set the type attribute to text, the text for the password was displayed in the box. That isn't very secure! What happens if the Bond Brothers are nearby when Dr. Day types in the password?

If we want to keep our password secret, we can change the value of our type attribute to password. This will hide what the user types by changing the text to dots. Let's take a look:

```
<body>
  <p style="font-size: 30pt;">THE MONK DIAMOND DISCOVERY</p>
  <p>Please enter the password to view this website.</p>
  <p>Password:<input id="passwordBox" type="password"/></p>
  <a href="monkdiamonddiscovery.html">
    Click here to submit password and view website
  </a>
</body>
```

password value

That's a much better way of keeping the password secret!

Password ✖   ✖

THE MONK DIAMOND DISCOVERY

Please enter the password to view this website.

Password: •••••••••

Click here to submit password and view website

Using JavaScript to check the Password

Now that we've built the basic HTML structure of our page, we need to write some JavaScript that will check whether the password the user enters is correct. If they enter the password Ernest300, they will be taken to the Monk Diamond Discovery page. If they enter an incorrect password, an alert will pop up telling them they have gotten the password wrong.

The first thing we need to do is create a function that will contain all the code we need to check our password. Let's create the function inside our <head>. You can put JavaScript anywhere in an HTML web page, and having it in our <head> in this example makes our code easier to understand. Don't forget to put your JavaScript inside the <script> tag, like this:

```
<script>
    function checkPassword() {
    }
</script>
```
function

We then need to create variables that store the value of our password, so that our function can check whether the user has the correct one. Let's look at the two variables we need:

```
<script>
    function checkPassword() {
        var password = document.getElementById("passwordBox");
        var passwordText = password.value;
    }
</script>
```
variable 1
variable 2
getElementById
id attribute

In our first variable, we are using a new built-in function called getElementById. You will learn all about this function and use it more in Mission 3. It is a handy function that finds the HTML element with the specified id attribute. The id attribute we have selected here is for our <input/> tag. So the value of our variable will be whatever data the user has typed into the password box.

We then create a second variable to store the data that the user has typed into the password box. We create this value by typing the name of our first variable followed by a dot (.) and then the value keyword. We do this so we can write an if statement using the value of this variable.

We now need to create an if statement. If the condition of our second variable is true and our password text is equal to (==) Ernest300, the hyperlink will work. If the condition of our variable is false and the password text is not equal to Ernest300, the link won't work and an alert will pop up. We don't need to use an else statement because the return statement will halt the function.

Turn the page to see what that code looks like!

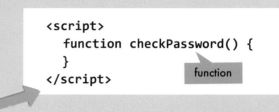

Our complete `<script>` block for our password with the new if statement looks like this:

```
<script>
  function checkPassword() {
    var password = document.getElementById("passwordBox");
    var passwordText = password.value;
    if(passwordText == "Ernest300") {
      return true;
    }
    alert("Access denied! Incorrect password!");
    return false;
  }
</script>
```

if statement

alert

Finally, we have to make our JavaScript work with our HTML elements. We need to look at the code in the `<body>` of our page now. We want to call the checkPassword function when someone clicks on the hyperlink in our page. So we need to add an onclick attribute to our opening `<a>` tag, like this:

```
<body>
  <p style="font-size: 30pt;">THE MONK DIAMOND DISCOVERY</p>
  <p>Please enter the password to view this website.</p>
  <p>Password:<input id="passwordBox" type="password"/></p>
  <a href="monkdiamonddiscovery.html" onclick="return checkPassword();">
    Click here to submit password and view website
  </a>
</body>
```

function call

Incorrect password

Correct password

THE MONK DIAMOND DISCOVERY

Please enter the password to view this website.

Password: ●●●●●●●●

Click here to submit password and view website

Access denied! Incorrect password!

OK

The Monk Diamond Discovery

Stolen Diamond Discovered in Siberia!

Mission 2

DO-IT-YOURSELF TASK
CREATE A PASSWORD

It's time to try using all the JavaScript Code Skills you've learned in this mission to create a new web page that asks the user to enter a password. This web page will protect the web page you built in Mission 1. If the user gets the password right, they will be able to access the Monk Diamond Discovery web page. If they get it wrong, an alert will pop up telling them that access is denied.

The Monk Diamond Discovery Password Brief

When you build your new web page, make sure you code these things using HTML and JavaScript:

- **A function** that will check your password when it is called
- **Variables** that will store the value of the data the user enters into the password box
- **An if statement** that will check whether the password the user enters is correct
- **An alert** that will pop up if an incorrect password is entered
- **A text box** the user can enter data into
- **A hyperlink** that connects this web page to the Monk Diamond Discovery web page

Save your file in your **Coding** folder and call it **password.html**.

> Turn the page to see the code you need for your password page.

```
<!DOCTYPE html>
<html>
<head>
   <title>Password</title>
   <style>
     body {
        background-color: lightblue;
        padding: 30px;
     }
   </style>
   <script>
     function checkPassword() {
        var password = document.getElementById("passwordBox");
        var passwordText = password.value;
        if(passwordText == "Ernest300") {
           return true;
        }
        alert("Access denied! Incorrect password!");
        return false;
     }
   </script>
</head>
<body>
   <p style="font-size: 30pt;">THE MONK DIAMOND DISCOVERY</p>
   <p>Please enter the password to view this website.</p>
   <p>Password:<input id="passwordBox" type="password"/></p>
   <a href="monkdiamonddiscovery.html" onclick="return
     checkPassword();">
     Click here to submit password and view website
   </a>
</body>
</html>
```

The Bond Brothers won't beat us!

Password ✖ ✖

THE MONK DIAMOND DISCOVERY

Please enter the password to view this website.

Password: •••••••••

Click here to submit password and view website

Brilliant coding! This password page will keep the Monk Diamond safe. Don't forget that you can use more CSS properties to change the look of the page.

FUTURE CODE SKILLS

JavaScript is a powerful and dynamic programming language, used by all modern web browsers. Knowing JavaScript allows you to create interactive and responsive web pages that allow a user to enter information. It's also great for building web-based apps.

BUILD AN APP

- CREATE A BUTTON USING JAVASCRIPT

- PROGRAM YOUR WEB BROWSER USING THE DOCUMENT OBJECT MODEL (DOM) API

- LEARN TO MAKE YOUR WEB PAGE REMEMBER THINGS WITH THE LOCALSTORAGE API

- BUILD A TO-DO LIST APP

Dear Coder,

You'll be pleased to hear that there are no more suspicious events to report. I think that the work you did for Dr. Day has been a success, and, unable to access our web page, the Bond Brothers have been thrown off our trail. Once again you impress me!

My injured ankle has now healed. We left the mountains yesterday and are currently on the Trans-Siberian Railway to Moscow. Our first-class train car is very luxurious, and I've been e-mailing my old and dear friend Mr. Viktor Volkov of the House of Volkov. As you already know, the Monk Diamond was audaciously stolen from the House of Volkov three years ago. It is one of the oldest and most respected jewelry companies in the world, and Mr. Volkov was devastated by the theft.

I have told Mr. Volkov about our discovery. At first he couldn't believe it! But finally I convinced him, and he wants us to return to Moscow with the diamond as quickly as possible. He is already making plans for a special exhibition. He will invite the most important jewel collectors from all over the world and announce our discovery.

Mr. Volkov needs help with planning the exhibition. Since we're on the train, I was hoping once again you might be able to help. Is there any way you could build a to-do list app? We can use the app to keep track of all the different tasks we need to do between now and the opening of the exhibition. I can be quite absentminded, so having the app would be really useful.

If we don't plan the exhibition properly (and with maximum security), I'm worried that the Bond Brothers might try to steal back the diamond. I'm attaching some notes about what needs to be done before the opening of the exhibition and also an entry from the Explorer's Encyclopedia about the House of Volkov, which will help you build the app.

Warmest regards from my comfortable train car,
Professor Harry Bairstone

The House of Volkov

From the Explorer's Encyclopedia: The Guide to Every Adventure

THE EXPLORER'S
ENCYCLOPEDIA
The Guide to Every Adventure

Home page
Contents
Featured discoveries
Famous explorers
Historical expeditions

Volkov Diamonds redirects here.

The **House of Volkov** is one of the world's oldest jewelry stores, famous for its high-quality diamond jewelry. It also has a world-renowned private collection of gems.

The House of Volkov was founded in St. Petersburg in the 1790s by Vladimir Volkov, who became known as the Prince of Diamonds for his love of the most rare and valuable stones. The House of Volkov was appointed the official

The Monk Diamond Special Exhibition
To-Do List

- Commission a state-of-the-art unbreakable glass display case
- Order a new velvet cushion for the diamond
- Hire private security
- Hire a bodyguard to protect Mr. Volkov
- Invite guests
- Buy diamond-themed snacks and lemonade
- Buy dog biscuits for Ernest

jeweler of the Imperial Court, supplying the Russian nobility with beautiful jewelry in intricate designs.

Today the House of Volkov is located on one of the most exclusive streets in Moscow, near St. Basil's Cathedral. Volkov diamonds are still renowned for their quality and are some of the most expensive in the world.

Viktor Volkov, the current owner, bought the Monk Diamond for an undisclosed sum at auction. It was the centerpiece of the House of Volkov's private collection. It was displayed to the public in an antique glass case until it was stolen in a smash-and-grab robbery. The theft of the Monk Diamond remains unsolved. Since the robbery, the House of Volkov has reported a sharp drop in sales, and there are rumors that it might be sold. Mr. Volkov said in a recent interview, "I would be devastated if the business, which has been in my family for generations, had to close."

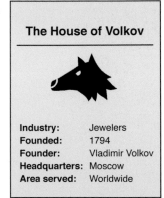

The House of Volkov

Industry:	Jewelers
Founded:	1794
Founder:	Vladimir Volkov
Headquarters:	Moscow
Area served:	Worldwide

BUILDING A WEB-BASED APP

Planning the special exhibition for the Monk Diamond at the House of Volkov is going to be a big job for Professor Bairstone, Dr. Day, and Mr. Volkov. In this mission you are going to help them by building an app that will run in your web browser. Professor Bairstone can use this app to create his to-do list. Once he's done a task, he can remove it from the list.

We're going to need to learn some new JavaScript functions to build our app. At the moment, the web pages we've built don't change after your browser has drawn them on-screen. Professor Bairstone is going to want to add and remove items from his list, so our app needs to be more interactive. Let's see what our app will look like:

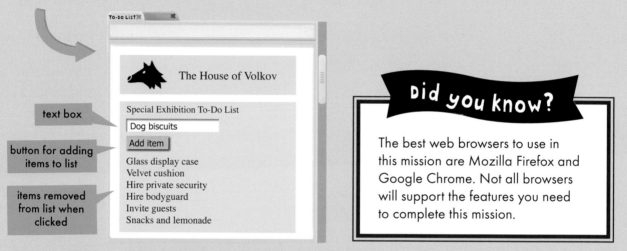

text box

button for adding items to list

items removed from list when clicked

The House of Volkov

Special Exhibition To-Do List

Dog biscuits

Add item

Glass display case
Velvet cushion
Hire private security
Hire bodyguard
Invite guests
Snacks and lemonade

Did you know?

The best web browsers to use in this mission are Mozilla Firefox and Google Chrome. Not all browsers will support the features you need to complete this mission.

Our app will have a text box that Professor Bairstone can type into. When he clicks on the button, the item will be added to the list. When he's completed a task, he can click on it again and it will be removed. We can code all these things using the JavaScript you learned in Mission 2 with some new programming tools.

Building a Text Box and Button

Before we start learning new JavaScript code, let's build the basic structure of our app. We need a text box and a button. In Mission 2, you learned how to use the `<input/>` tag and the type attribute. We're going to be using those skills again in this mission.

The `<input/>` tag allows you to create an HTML element on your page where your user can enter data. You use the type attribute to choose the kind of element your user can add data to. So to create a text box and a clickable button on our page, we will need the following code:

```
<input type="text"/>
<input type="button"/>
```

We also need to add some text inside the text box and button, so the user knows what action they perform. We do this by adding a new value attribute to the `<input/>` tags:

```
<input type="text" value="Type here to add task"/>
<input type="button" value="Add item"/>
```

Then we can change the CSS properties of our `<input/>` tags to make them look a bit more exciting. We do this with CSS classes, like we did in Mission 1. But this time, rather than giving our CSS class a name, we use the CSS type attribute selector to find and format our button. Let's look at the whole code block:

```
<!DOCTYPE html>
<html>
<head>
  <title>To-Do List App</title>
  <style>
    input[type="button"] {
      background-color: pink;
    }
  </style>
</head>
<body>
  <p>Special Exhibition To-Do List</p>
  <br/>
  <input type="text" value="Type here to add task"/>
  <br/>
  <input type="button" value="Add item"/>
  <br/>
</body>
</html>
```

This is the CSS type attribute selector. It finds the selected type attribute and then formats it to your chosen CSS properties.

type attribute

But if you try to type into the text box or click the button, nothing will happen. If we want our button and text box to work, we need to add some JavaScript to our page.

CODE SKILLS ► HOW TO BUILD A BUTTON

Let's start making the app for Professor Bairstone by building a button. Use <input/> tags to code a text box and button.

1. Open up your text-editing program. Create a new HTML file called **app.html**. Type this code into your new file:

```
<!DOCTYPE html>
<html>
<head>
   <title>To-Do List App</title>
</head>
<body>
   <p>Special Exhibition To-Do List</p>
   <br/>
   <br/>
   <br/>
</body>
</html>
```

2. Now use the <input/> tag to create a text box and button in your <body>. Don't forget that you need to include two attributes inside your <input/> tags: the type and value attributes. You should set the value attribute to the text you want to display in your box and button. Your code will look like this:

```
<body>
   <p>Special Exhibition To-Do List</p>
   <br/>
   <input type="text" value="Type here to add task"/>
   <br/>
   <input type="button" value="Add item"/>
   <br/>
</body>
```

3. Save your HTML file and open it in your browser. You will see your box and button displayed on-screen.

   Now create a CSS class and use the CSS type attribute selector to change the color of your button.

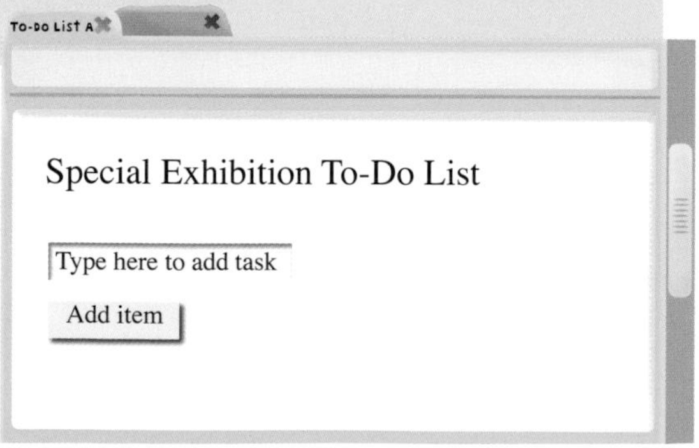

To-Do List A
Special Exhibition To-Do List
Type here to add task
Add item

3

Making Buttons Run Code

We now need to make the button in our app interactive. To make the button run JavaScript code when we click it, we need to add the onclick attribute to our button <input/> tag, like we did in Mission 2. When the user clicks on the button, we want it to call a JavaScript function. All we have to do is set the value of our onclick attribute to the name of the function we want to call.

Let's code a button that will call a function that pops up an alert when it's clicked. First create the JavaScript function you need. Then add the onclick attribute to the <input/> tag for the button. Finally, set the value of the onclick attribute to the name of the function. Do this by using the equals sign (=) and double quotes (" "). The code we need looks like this:

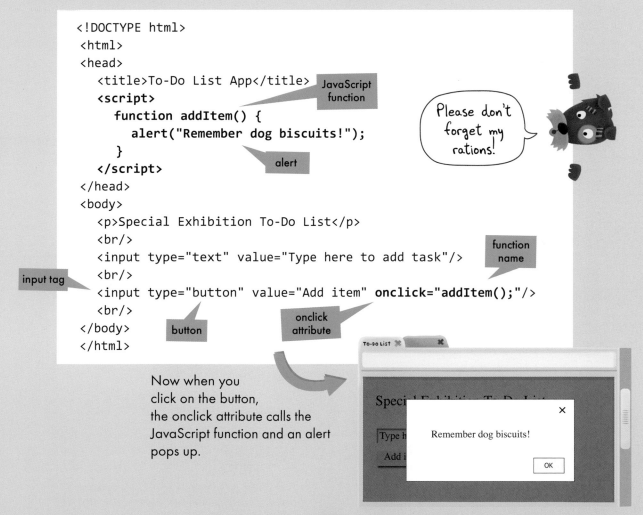

```
<!DOCTYPE html>
<html>
<head>
    <title>To-Do List App</title>        JavaScript function
    <script>
      function addItem() {
         alert("Remember dog biscuits!");
      }                                    alert
    </script>
</head>
<body>
    <p>Special Exhibition To-Do List</p>
    <br/>
    <input type="text" value="Type here to add task"/>   function name
    <br/>
    <input type="button" value="Add item" onclick="addItem();"/>   input tag
    <br/>
</body>                button     onclick attribute
</html>
```

Please don't forget my rations!

Now when you click on the button, the onclick attribute calls the JavaScript function and an alert pops up.

TO-DO LIST

Special Exhibition To-Do List

Remember dog biscuits!   ✕

Type h

Add i   OK

Now practice using the onclick attribute to make a button that pops up an alert.

1. Open up your text-editing program. Create a new HTML file called **button.html**. Then copy and paste your code from **app.html** into your new file. In your <body> add an onclick attribute that calls a JavaScript function to your button, like this:

```
<!DOCTYPE html>
<html>
<head>
    <title>To-Do List App</title>
</head>
<body>
    <p>Special Exhibition To-Do List App</p>
    <br/>
    <input type="text" value="Type here to add task"/>
    <br/>
    <input type="button" value="Add item" onclick="addItem();"/>
    <br/>
</body>
</html>
```

2. Add the <script> tag to your <head>. Create a JavaScript function that will pop up an alert when it's called. Your code will look like this:

```
<head>
    <title>To-Do List App</title>
    <script>
      function addItem() {
        alert("Hire security team!");
      }
    </script>
</head>
```

3. Save your HTML file and open it in your browser. Your button will now pop up an alert when you click on it.

THE DOCUMENT OBJECT MODEL (DOM)

The button and text box in our app now work. But how will Professor Bairstone add and remove items from his list? To allow him to do this, we need to use the Document Object Model (or DOM for short).

We learned in Mission 1 that an HTML web page file is called a document. As you know, HTML documents are made up of lots of smaller pieces of HTML, called HTML elements. When we save our HTML file and run the code in our web browser, the browser draws the elements on-screen. If we want

to build the app, we need to be able to change, delete, or add new HTML elements after our browser has drawn the page on our screen.

As we've seen working through Mission 2, built-in functions such as the alert are very useful when we code. The DOM is a set of built-in functions that work with your web browser. The built-in functions make it easy to build web pages that are dynamic, changing according to what the user does.

Programming Interfaces

The DOM is an **application program interface** (or **API**). APIs help when you are coding. They are sets of built-in functions that you can easily use with your HTML and JavaScript code.

The DOM will help make your app interactive.

The alert function we used in Mission 2 is a built-in function. Rather than having to code an alert, we can just type the alert keyword, and our browser knows what to do. The DOM works in a very similar way. We can use the DOM's built-in functions to make changes to our HTML document after it's been drawn on-screen.

Using the DOM lets us build web pages that change and react when the user does something. So if we want our to-do list to be interactive and change on-screen when Professor Bairstone adds a new task or checks one off, we need to use the DOM's methods and properties.

CODE WORDS

APPLICATION PROGRAM INTERFACES (APIs) save lots of time when you are writing code, because they allow you to use their built-in functions. Rather than having to write the code for these functions yourself, you can use the API's functions in your code. There are APIs to do all sorts of things, from storing information to adding content to your page.

Using the DOM

The DOM API is structured in a special way called a hierarchy, which is a bit like a family tree. This structure is called the document object. In the document object the individual HTML elements are all connected to one another, like the members of a family, with parents and children. The way the document object is structured allows you to use another programming language, such as JavaScript, to access, change, add, or remove any of the HTML elements inside the document.

Using the DOM when you code allows you to make changes to individual HTML elements after they have been drawn on-screen. You can use the DOM's methods and properties to find an HTML element on your page and then, using JavaScript, add to it, remove it, or change it.

If we want our app to be interactive, we need to learn how to use these methods and properties with JavaScript. Professor Bairstone needs to be able to see his tasks on-screen and then add and remove items.

DOM Methods and Properties

Before you can use any of the DOM's built-in functions, you have to tell your browser you want to access the API. To do this, you always have to type this piece of code at the beginning of an instruction for the DOM.

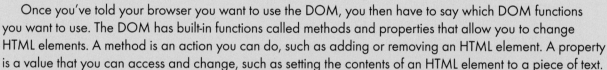

Once you've told your browser you want to use the DOM, you then have to say which DOM functions you want to use. The DOM has built-in functions called methods and properties that allow you to change HTML elements. A method is an action you can do, such as adding or removing an HTML element. A property is a value that you can access and change, such as setting the contents of an HTML element to a piece of text.

When you want to use a method or property, you separate the DOM keyword from the DOM method or property with a dot (.). Because the DOM lets you access any HTML element in your web page, lots of DOM methods have the word "element" in them. In Mission 2, you used a DOM method with JavaScript when you wrote this code:

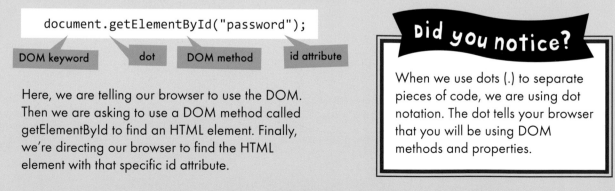

Here, we are telling our browser to use the DOM. Then we are asking to use a DOM method called getElementById to find an HTML element. Finally, we're directing our browser to find the HTML element with that specific id attribute.

Did you notice?

When we use dots (.) to separate pieces of code, we are using dot notation. The dot tells your browser that you will be using DOM methods and properties.

changing Your App with the DOM

We can use a DOM method to find an HTML element in our app by its id attribute. We can then use a DOM property to change the contents of that element. Let's look at how we do this.

Using the getElementById Method

The getElementById method is a very handy way of finding a specific HTML element in your block of code. To use the getElementById method, you have to include the id attribute you gave to the HTML element in parentheses after the keyword, like this:

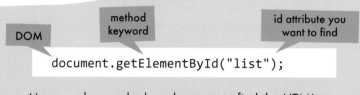

```
document.getElementById("list");
```

Here, we have asked our browser to find the HTML element in our web page that has the id attribute set to the value "list".

Using the innerHTML Property

You can use the DOM's innerHTML property to access or change the contents of an HTML element in your app. You can then use the contents of the HTML element as a value in your JavaScript code.

```
var showList = document.getElementById("list");
alert(showList.innerHTML);
```

Here, we have created a variable where the value is set to the contents of the HTML element that we have called "list", using the id attribute. We have then created an alert. The alert will pop up the value of our variable. Our browser can access this information because we have set the innerHTML property of the variable.

The DOM is case sensitive. Make sure your capital letters are in the right place.

Turn the page to see how you can use this method and property.

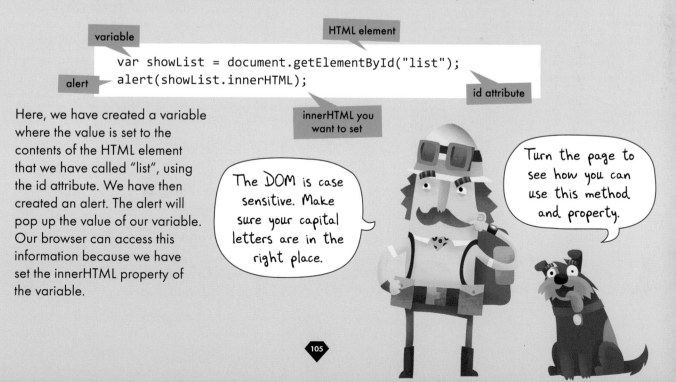

Let's look at using the getElementById method with the innerHTML property to pop up an alert:

```
<!DOCTYPE html>
<html>
<head>
  <title>List Alert</title>
</head>
<body>
  <div id="list">Buy Ernest a new collar</div>
  <script>
    var showList = document.getElementById("list");
    alert(showList.innerHTML);
  </script>
</body>
</html>
```

id attribute

innerHTML property

getElementById method

In this example, we've used the getElementById method to find the <div> with the id attribute set to "list". You will remember <div> tags from Mission 1. They are containers for pieces of content, and you can use them to divide your page into sections.

We've then stored the contents of that <div> in a variable. Then we've used innerHTML to set the text in our alert to the value of our variable. If the text in the <div> changes, so will the text inside the alert box, without our having to write any more code.

List Alert

Buy Ernest a new collar

Buy Ernest a new collar

×

OK

Pawsome list!

CODE SKILLS ► METHODS AND PROPERTIES

Let's try using the getElementById method and the innerHTML property to find and change the contents of an HTML element.

1. Open up your text-editing program. Create a new HTML file called **methods.html**. In your <body> use the <input/> tag to create a button. Also create an empty <div>, like this:

2. Now create a JavaScript function in your <head> that uses the getElementById method to find your empty <div>. Then use innerHTML to set the contents of your empty <div> to some text, like this:

```
<!DOCTYPE html>
<html>
<head>
    <title>Methods</title>
</head>
<body>
    <input type="button" value="Add item"/>
    <div id="container"></div>
</body>
</html>
```

```
<script>
    function addItem() {
        document.getElementById("container").innerHTML = "Item to remember";
    }
</script>
```

3. Next, make your button call your JavaScript function when it is clicked. Add the onclick attribute to your <input/> tag and set the value of the onclick attribute to the name of your function, like this:

```
<input type="button" value="Add item" onclick="addItem();"/>
<div id="container"></div>
```

4. Save your HTML file and open it in your browser. You will see a button. When you click on the button, the innerHTML text will be added to your <div>.

Methods

Add item

Item to remember

Adding to Your App Using the DOM

We now know how to use the DOM's methods and properties to find and change HTML elements in our app, which will be really useful. We now need to learn how to use the DOM to add new HTML elements to our app. After all, Professor Bairstone needs to be able to add items to the list. The DOM has two methods that we can use with JavaScript to do this.

The createElement Method

The createElement method is used to make a new HTML element, such as a `<div>`, button, or paragraph. You have to include the name of the type of HTML element you want to create in double quotes (" ") and parentheses after the keyword, like this:

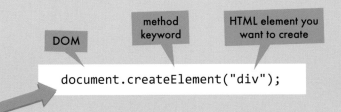

DOM • method keyword • HTML element you want to create

```
document.createElement("div");
```

You can then use JavaScript to assign your new element to a variable, using the assignment operator (=) we learned about in Mission 2. Then you can use the innerHTML property to set the content of your new element before your browser draws it on-screen.

The appendChild Method

The appendChild method lets you add a new HTML element to an existing HTML element. When the new element is drawn on-screen, it will be drawn underneath the existing element. You have to include the HTML element you want to add in parentheses after the keyword, like this:

```
<script>
  var newDiv = document.createElement("div");
  newDiv.innerHTML = "Professor Bairstone";
  document.body.appendChild(newDiv);
</script>
```

create `<div>` • set innerHTML • location • appendChild

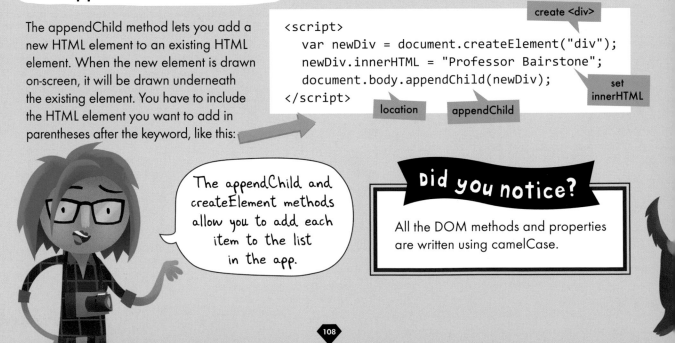

The appendChild and createElement methods allow you to add each item to the list in the app.

Did you notice?

All the DOM methods and properties are written using camelCase.

Let's look at an example that uses the createElement and appendChild methods to create a new HTML element on our page. The HTML element will be a `<div>` with a piece of text inside it. A `<div>` is a useful way of creating a section or container for other HTML elements.

```
<!DOCTYPE html>
<html>
<head>
  <title>To-Do List App</title>
</head>
<body>
  <div id="list">To-Do List</div>
  <script>
    var newItem = document.createElement("div");
    newItem.innerHTML = "Item added to list";
    document.getElementById("list").appendChild(newItem);
  </script>
</body>
</html>
```

id attribute

createElement

create `<div>`

variable

appendChild

add HTML element

The first thing we've done is code a `<div>` and set its id attribute to list. This `<div>` will be the HTML element we add our new HTML element to, using appendChild.

Then we've opened the `<script>` tag and created a block of JavaScript code. In the first line of JavaScript, we have used createElement to make a `<div>`. We have then stored this new `<div>` in a variable called newItem. You can use any name you want here.

In our next line of JavaScript, we've set the value of our variable to a piece of text using the innerHTML property. Our new `<div>`, stored in our variable, now contains text.

To-Do List
Item added to list

In our final line of JavaScript, we've used getElementById to find the first `<div>` we made using the id attribute. We've then used appendChild to add the `<div>` stored in our variable to the first `<div>` on our page.

When we run our code in our web browser, we will see that our new `<div>` has been added to our first `<div>`.

You wouldn't believe how forgetful Professor Bairstone can be!

109

Now it's your turn to try using the createElement and appendChild methods. In your code, use the DOM and JavaScript to create a new HTML element when an existing element is clicked. Using APIs like the DOM makes building apps easier.

1. Open up your text-editing program. Create a new HTML file called **newelements.html**. Code a `<div>` (with an id attribute) that contains text, like this:

```
<!DOCTYPE html>
<html>
<head>
   <title>New Elements</title>
</head>
<body>
   <div id="list">Click here to add item</div>
</body>
</html>
```

2. In your `<head>`, create a new function. Your code will look like this:

```
<head>
   <title>New Elements</title>
   <script>
      function addItem() {
      }
   </script>
</head>
```

3. Now make your function create a new `<div>` using the createElement method. Store your new `<div>` in a variable and give the variable a name. Then set the value of your new `<div>` to some text using the innerHTML property. Your code will look like this:

```
<script>
   function addItem() {
      var newItem = document.createElement("div");
      newItem.innerHTML = "New item";
   }
</script>
```

4. Add a final line to your function. Use getElementById to find the <div> in your <body>. Use the appendChild method to add the new <div> to the <div> in your <body>. Your code will look like this:

```
<script>
  function addItem() {
    var newItem = document.createElement("div");
    newItem.innerHTML = "New item";
    document.getElementById("list").appendChild(newItem);
  }
</script>
```

5. Now the only thing missing is the function call in the <body> of your code. Add the onclick attribute to the <div> in your <body>, so that when the <div> text is clicked, your addItem function is called. Your code will look like this:

```
<body>
  <div id="list" onclick="addItem();">Click here to add item</div>
</body>
```

6. Save your HTML file and open it in your browser. When you click on the "Click here" piece of text, a new <div> will be added to your app every time you click.

New Elemen

Click here to add item
New item
New item
New item
New item
New item
New item

But how do we add the button to the app?

Turn the page to find out!

MAKING THE TO-DO LIST APP

Now that you know what the DOM is and how it works, let's bring together all your new Code Skills and create the to-do list app. At the start of the mission, you learned how to build a text box and button using the <input/> tag. Let's look at that code again:

```
<!DOCTYPE html>
<html>
<head>
   <title>To-Do List App</title>
</head>
<body>
   <p>Special Exhibition To-Do List</p>
   <br/>
   <input type="text" value="Type here to add task"/>        text box
   <br/>
   <input type="button" value="Add item"/>        button
   <br/>
</body>
</html>
```

At the moment, Professor Bairstone can type a task into the text box, but when he clicks on the button, nothing happens. We have to use the DOM's methods and properties to add an item to the list when the button is clicked.

Let's start with the changes we need to make to our <body>. We need to add an onclick attribute to our <input/> tag to make our button work. This onclick has to call a function. We also need to create an empty <div> that will become our to-do list. When an item is added to the list, it will be added to this empty <div> using the DOM methods. Our <body> block will look like this:

112

```
<body>
  <p>Special Exhibition To-Do List</p>
  <br/>
  <input type="text" value="Type here to add task"/>
  <br/>
  <input type="button" value="Add item" onclick="addItem();"/>
  <br/>
  <div id="list"></div>           <div>
</body>
```

onclick attribute

Now let's create a function in our <head> that will run when the onclick is clicked. Our function needs to use the createElement method to make a new <div>. This new <div> will be stored in a variable called newItem. Then we need to use innerHTML to set the text inside our newItem variable. Finally, we need to use getElementById to find the <div> with the id attribute "list" in our body. Then we can use appendChild to add our newItem to our list. Our <script> block in our <head> will look like this:

```
<script>
  function addItem() {
    var newItem = document.createElement("div");
    newItem.innerHTML = "New item";
    document.getElementById("list").appendChild(newItem);
  }
</script>
```

create new <div>

set innerHTML of new <div>

find id attribute

add new <div> to <div> in <body>

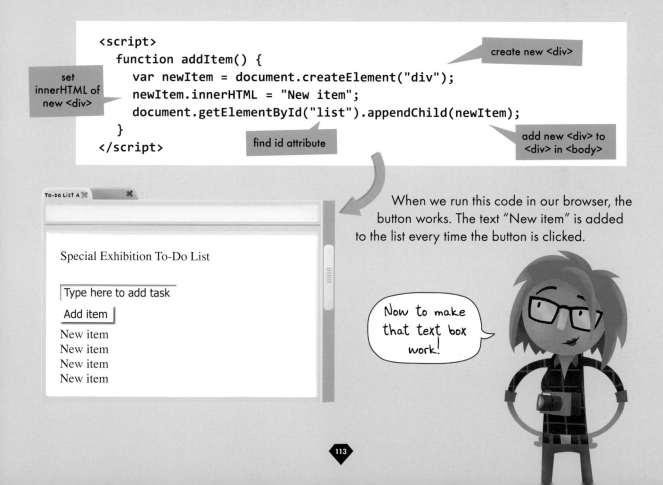

When we run this code in our browser, the button works. The text "New item" is added to the list every time the button is clicked.

TO-DO LIST A

Special Exhibition To-Do List

Type here to add task

Add item

New item
New item
New item
New item

Now to make that text box work!

Adding Your Own Tasks

Our app is really starting to take shape. Now an item is added to the list every time the user clicks the button. But Professor Bairstone can't yet type an item into the text box and add it to the list. Let's see how we can allow him to type in his own tasks.

We only need to change two lines in our code block to add the value of the text box to the list. The first thing we need to do is in our <body>. We need to give the <input/> tag for our text box an id attribute of our choice, like this:

id attribute

```
<input type="text" id="box" value="Type here to add task"/>
```

We're then going to change our JavaScript in the <head> so that it sets the innerHTML of the new <div> to whatever value has been typed into the text box. To do that, we have to use getElementById to find the text box using the id attribute. We then access the value by making this change to our <script> block:

```
<script>
  function addItem() {
    var newItem = document.createElement("div");
    newItem.innerHTML = document.getElementById("box").value;
    document.getElementById("list").appendChild(newItem);
  }
</script>
```

id attribute

access value

Now Professor Bairstone can replace the text in the text box with the item he wants to add to his list. Our addItem function will set whatever text is typed into the text box as the contents of the new <div>. He can now add his own items to the to-do list.

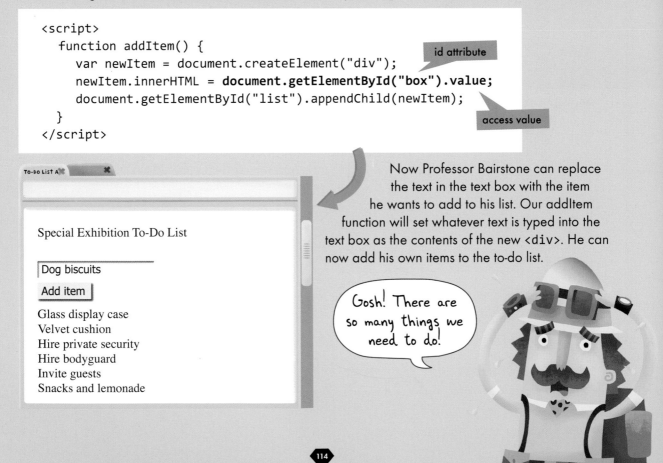

Special Exhibition To-Do List

Dog biscuits

Add item

Glass display case
Velvet cushion
Hire private security
Hire bodyguard
Invite guests
Snacks and lemonade

Gosh! There are so many things we need to do!

code skills checklist ✔

USING THE DOM API

- The DOM (or Document Object Model) is an API (Application Program Interface). When your HTML document runs in your web browser, it becomes a part of the DOM called the document object. The way the document object is structured allows you to write code that will access and change individual HTML elements.

- You can use the DOM's built-in functions to make changes to HTML elements after they have been drawn on your screen. This is important if you want to make an interactive web page or web-based app that responds to the user.

- To access the DOM, you have to type the document keyword. You also have to use dot (.) notation. Each new instruction for the DOM has to be separated by a dot.

- You can use DOM methods and properties to make changes to your HTML elements.

- getElementById is a DOM method that allows you to find an HTML element on your page by its id attribute.

- innerHTML is a DOM property. You can set the innerHTML of any HTML element. Using innerHTML is a good way to set or change the contents of an HTML element.

- createElement is a DOM method that lets you create a new HTML element. You have to tell your browser what type of element you want to create.

- appendChild is a DOM method that lets you add a new HTML element to an existing HTML element.

> The DOM saves you lots of time and makes it much easier to create a dynamic web page!

CODE SKILLS ► BUILDING THE BASIC APP

Let's build a basic app. The app should have a text box and a button that Professor Bairstone can use to add his tasks to the list. Use the DOM and JavaScript so that when the button is clicked, the task in the box will be added to the list.

1. Open up your text-editing program. Create a new HTML file called **basicapp.html**. Then copy and paste your code from **app.html** into your new file. Modify your code so that the text box has an id attribute of your choice, like this:

```
<!DOCTYPE html>
<html>
<head>
  <title>To-Do List App</title>
</head>
<body>
  <p>Special Exhibition To-Do List</p>
  <br/>
  <input type="text" id="box" value="Type here to add task"/>
  <br/>
  <input type="button" value="Add item"/>
  <br/>
</body>
</html>
```

Don't forget to set the id attribute!

2. Add an empty `<div>` at the bottom of your `<body>`. Give your `<div>` an id attribute of your choice, like this:

```
<input type="button" value="Add item"/>
<br/>
<div id="list"></div>
```

3. Now add an onclick attribute to your button `<input/>` tag. Set your onclick to call a JavaScript function. Your code will look like this:

```
<input type="button" value="Add item" onclick="addItem();"/>
```

4. Add an empty JavaScript function to your <head>. Your <script> block needs to look like this:

```
<head>
  <title>To-Do List App</title>
  <script>
    function addItem() {
    }
  </script>
</head
```

5. Now use the DOM to code a function called addItem that will create a new <div> when the button is clicked. The function will then use innerHTML to set the value of the <div> to the value in the text box. Finally, the function will use appendChild to add the new HTML element to the <div> in your <body>. Your code will look like this:

```
<script>
  function addItem() {
    var newItem = document.createElement("div");
    newItem.innerHTML = document.getElementById("box").value;
    document.getElementById("list").appendChild(newItem);
  }
</script>
```

6. Save your HTML file and open it in your browser. You will now be able to replace the text in the text box with an item for the list. When you click on the button, the item typed into the text box will be added to the list.

Special Exhibition To-Do List

Velvet cushion

Add item

Glass display case

Great work! I can add all my tasks to the list now!

dog biscuits

Removing Elements from the App

You know how to use the DOM to find and add HTML elements to your web page. But what happens if Professor Bairstone makes a mistake and adds the wrong item to the to-do list? Or if he completes a task and wants to remove it from the list? We need to learn how to remove HTML elements from our app using the DOM.

> Imagine if I added that new pair of woolly socks I need to the list! Terrible!

The removeChild Method

The removeChild method does the opposite of the appendChild method. Rather than adding an HTML element to another HTML element, it takes away an HTML element from another HTML element. You use it just like appendChild. Select the HTML element you want to remove using the id attribute, and then tell your browser to remove it, like this:

find parent HTML element   **remove child HTML element**

```
document.getElementById("list").removeChild(this);
```

As you know already, HTML tags can be nested inside other HTML tags. When you use the removeChild method, you remove the HTML element inside the HTML element you selected using the id attribute.

> These new pieces of code are making our app more and more interactive.

In the document object, all elements are connected, like in a family tree. Any HTML element that is inside another is called a child of that element. The HTML element on the outside is called the parent. When you use removeChild, you remove the child HTML element from the parent HTML element.

When you use the removeChild method, you also have to use a handy JavaScript keyword called "this". The this keyword points to whichever HTML element was used to call the function. Let's look at an example:

```
<!DOCTYPE html>
<html>
<head>
  <title>Things to Buy</title>
  <script>
    function removeItem(item) {                    argument
      document.getElementById("list").removeChild(item);
    }
  </script>
</head>
<body>
  <div id="list">                                   this keyword
parent <div>
      Velvet cushion for diamond
    <div onclick="removeItem(this);">
child <div>
        Woolly socks
    </div>
  </div>
</body>
</html>
```

In this example, the first <div>, with the id attribute "list", is the parent element. The <div> nested inside it, with the woolly socks text, is the child element. When we click on the woolly socks text, we're using getElementById to find the <div> called list.

Then we're using the removeChild method and the this keyword to remove this piece of text. Just like we learned in Mission 2, we have to pass an argument for our function to work. We use the argument "item" and the "this" keyword to keep track of the HTML element we are trying to remove. Professor Bairstone can now remove things from the list by clicking on them.

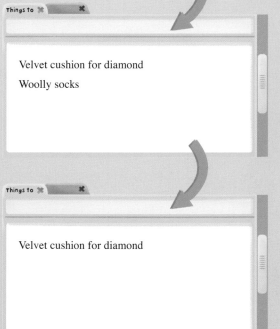

Silly Professor Bairstone!

CODE SKILLS ► REMOVING AN HTML ELEMENT

Let's try using the removeChild method and the this keyword to remove an HTML element.

1. Open up your text-editing program. Create a new HTML file called **remove.html**. Code a parent and a child `<div>` in your `<body>`. Set the id attribute of the parent `<div>`, like this:

```
<!DOCTYPE html>
<html>
<head>
    <title>Remove Items</title>
</head>
<body>
    <div id="list">
        Security to protect Mr. Volkov
        <div>
            Woolly socks
        </div>
    </div>
</body>
</html>
```

2. Now add a JavaScript function to your `<head>` that will remove the child `<div>` from your page. The function will find the parent `<div>` using the getElementById method. It will then use removeChild to remove the `<div>` nested inside it. Your code will look like this:

```
<script>
    function removeItem(item) {
        document.getElementById("list").removeChild(item);
    }
</script>
```

3. Finally, add an onclick attribute to the child `<div>`, so that when the text inside it is clicked, it will be removed from the list. The onclick should call your function and use the this keyword, like this:

```
<div onclick="removeItem(this);">
  Woolly socks
</div>
```

4. Save your HTML file and open it in your browser. When you click on the second item, it will vanish from the screen.

Removing More Than One HTML Element

You're making great progress! Now you can remove an HTML element using the removeChild method. But what happens if Professor Bairstone wants to remove more than one item from his list? We need to use the DOM and JavaScript so that all the items can be removed from the list when they're clicked. To do this we need to add an onclick attribute every time we use the createElement method. You can use a DOM method to set the onclick by using the onclick keyword:

`.onclick`

We can then set our onclick to call a function that will remove the item when it is clicked, like this:

```
<!DOCTYPE html>
<html>
<head>
    <title>To-Do List App</title>
    <script>
      function addItem() {
        var newItem = document.createElement("div");
        newItem.innerHTML = document.getElementById("box").value;
        newItem.onclick = removeItem;
        document.getElementById("list").appendChild(newItem);
      }
      function removeItem() {
        document.getElementById("list").removeChild(this);
      }
    </script>
</head>
<body>
    <p>Special Exhibition To-Do List</p>
    <input type="text" id="box" value="Type here to add task"/>
    <br/>
    <input type="button" value="Add item" onclick="addItem();"/>
    <div id="list"></div>
</body>
</html>
```

We need to get all these tasks checked off the list!

onclick attribute set

removeItem function called

In this example, we've created a new <div> using createElement. We've stored the <div> in a variable so we can set its innerHTML to whatever item has been typed into the text box. We then use the DOM to set the onclick attribute of the new item. When this item is clicked, it will call the removeItem function and the item will be removed from the list.

Use your new knowledge to make an app where more than one HTML element can be removed when it's clicked. Every new skill you learn is making your app more advanced.

I've got a bone to pick with those Bond Brothers! All this planning!

1. Open up your text-editing program. Create a new HTML file called **removemore.html**. Copy and paste your code from **basicapp.html**. Your code will look like this:

```html
<!DOCTYPE html>
<html>
<head>
   <title>To-Do List App</title>
   <script>
     function addItem() {
        var newItem = document.createElement("div");
        newItem.innerHTML = document.getElementById("box").value;
        document.getElementById("list").appendChild(newItem);
     }
   </script>
</head>
<body>
   <p>Special Exhibition To-Do List</p>
   <br/>
   <input type="text" id="box" value="Type here to add task"/>
   <br/>
   <input type="button" value="Add item" onclick="addItem();"/>
   <br/>
   <div id="list"></div>
</body>
</html>
```

2. Now modify your addItem function in your `<head>` by setting up the onclick attribute in your function. Add an onclick to every new HTML element. Make your onclick call a new function when it is clicked. Add this new line of code to your `<script>` block:

```
<script>
   function addItem() {
      var newItem = document.createElement("div");
      newItem.innerHTML = document.getElementById("box").value;
      newItem.onclick = removeItem;
      document.getElementById("list").appendChild(newItem);
   }
</script>
```

3. Code a second function in your `<script>` block called removeItem. The function needs to use getElementById to find the `<div>` in your `<body>`. Then it should use removeChild and the this keyword to remove any item the function calls. Type out this function so your `<script>` block now looks like this:

```
<script>
   function addItem() {
      var newItem = document.createElement("div");
      newItem.innerHTML = document.getElementById("box").value;
      newItem.onclick = removeItem;
      document.getElementById("list").appendChild(newItem);
   }
   function removeItem() {
      document.getElementById("list").removeChild(this);
   }
</script>
```

I'm Viktor Volkov. It's great to meet you. I can't tell you how grateful I am for your help. Your coding skills are very impressive.

4. Your finished code block for your app will look like this:

```
<!DOCTYPE html>
<html>
<head>
  <title>To-Do List App</title>
  <script>
    function addItem() {
      var newItem = document.createElement("div");
      newItem.innerHTML = document.getElementById("box").value;
      newItem.onclick = removeItem;
      document.getElementById("list").appendChild(newItem);
    }
    function removeItem() {
      document.getElementById("list").removeChild(this);
    }
  </script>
</head>
<body>
  <p>Special Exhibition To-Do List</p>
  <br/>
  <input type="text" id="box" value="Type here to add task"/>
  <br/>
  <input type="button" value="Add item" onclick="addItem();"/>
  <br/>
  <div id="list"></div>
</body>
</html>
```

This special exhibition is going to be a blast!

Save your HTML file and open it in your browser. You can now add and remove items from the list.

TO-DO List

Special Exhibition To-Do List

Add item

Glass display case
Velvet cushion
Hire private security
Woolly socks
Snacks and lemonade

TO-DO List

Special Exhibition To-Do List

Add item

Glass display case
Velvet cushion
Hire private security
Snacks and lemonade

SAVING YOUR TO-DO LIST ITEMS

Professor Bairstone can now add and remove as many items as he needs to and from the list. But you might have noticed that if you refresh your page, your to-do list disappears. This is because so far we've just added or removed HTML elements from our screen. We haven't saved the list or changed our HTML file. If we want our browser to save and remember our list, we need to use localStorage, a handy API that's available in HTML5 (the fifth version of the HTML programming language).

This API lets you save information in your browser, so even if your page is refreshed or closed, you can still access the data. Like the DOM, localStorage is a collection of functions, and it's simple to use.

All you have to do is tell your browser you want to use localStorage by typing the localStorage keyword (written in camelCase) and giving a name to the information you want to store. Set the value of the information you want to store using an equals sign (=) and double quotes (" "), like this:

> localStorage keyword · localStorage name · information stored

```
localStorage.storageName = "information";
```

If you want to remove a piece of information from localStorage, you just leave an empty value, like this:

> information removed

```
localStorage.storageName = "";
```

Viewing the information you save using localStorage is simple. All you have to do is use the keyword and the localStorage name, like this:

The Monk

The Monk Diamond

×

OK

```
<!DOCTYPE html>
<html>
<head>
  <title>The Monk Diamond</title>
</head>
<body>
  <script>
    localStorage.valuableDiamond = "The Monk Diamond";
    alert(localStorage.valuableDiamond);
  </script>
</body>
</html>
```

> keyword · name

Let's try using localStorage to store information in our web browser. This way the list in Professor Bairstone's app will be safely stored.

1. Open up your text-editing program. Create a new HTML file called **storage.html**. Type this code into the <body> of your new file:

```
<!DOCTYPE html>
<html>
<head>
   <title>Storage</title>
</head>
<body>
   <input type="text" id="box" value="Type here to add task"/><br/>
   <input type="button" id="save" value="Save" onclick="save();"/><br/>
   <input type="button" id="load" value="Load" onclick="load();"/><br/>
   Saved item: <div id="savedList"></div>
</body>
</html>
```

2. Now code a function in your <head> that uses localStorage to save the value typed into the text box in your browser. Don't forget to use camelCase when you write the localStorage keyword. Your code will look like this:

```
<script>
   function save() {
     var newItem = document.getElementById("box").value;
     localStorage.box = newItem;
   }
</script>
```

Don't forget to use Google Chrome or Mozilla Firefox for this exercise.

3. Now code a second function in your `<script>` block that uses the getElementById method to find your empty `<div>`. Use innerHTML to set the value of your empty `<div>` to the information you saved using localStorage. Make sure your function looks like this:

```
<script>
   function save() {
      var newItem = document.getElementById("box").value;
      localStorage.box = newItem;
   }
   function load() {
      var savedDiv = document.getElementById("savedList");
      savedDiv.innerHTML = localStorage.box;
   }
</script>
```

4. Save your HTML file and open it in your browser. Type something into the text box and click *Save*.

5. Now click *Load*. The value you typed into the text box will appear on-screen. Then refresh your page. The item will disappear from your screen. But when you press *Load*, the text you saved using localStorage will be loaded in your browser.

> Now, that is useful!

Did you notice?

When writing the localStorage keyword, we use camelCase. The first letter is lowercase, and the second word starts with an uppercase letter.

127

Saving and Loading Using localStorage

Now that you know about localStorage, let's look at how we can use it to save and load Professor Bairstone's app. Every time Professor Bairstone changes the to-do list, it needs to be saved in localStorage. We also need to write code that will load the to-do list from localStorage when Professor Bairstone opens it in his browser. Let's look at the changes we need to make to our `<script>` block to use localStorage like this:

```html
<!DOCTYPE html>
<html>
<head>
  <title>To-Do List App</title>
  <script>
    function addItem() {
      var newItem = document.createElement("div");
      newItem.innerHTML = document.getElementById("box").value;
      newItem.onclick = removeItem;
      document.getElementById("list").appendChild(newItem);
      saveList();
    }
    function removeItem() {
      document.getElementById("list").removeChild(this);
      saveList();
    }
    function saveList() {
      localStorage.storedList = document.getElementById("list").innerHTML;
    }
    function loadList() {
      document.getElementById("list").innerHTML = localStorage.storedList;
    }
  </script>
</head>
<body>
  <p>Special Exhibition To-Do List</p>
  <input type="text" id="box" value="Type here to add task"/>
  <br/>
  <input type="button" value="Add item" onclick="addItem();"/>
  <div id="list"></div>
</body>
</html>
```

save list function call

save list function call

list saved to localStorage

save list function

load list function

3

Saving the List

To save the list, we need to create a new saveList function that will save it using localStorage. To do this, we have to choose a variable name to assign the information we want to store in localStorage. We then use getElementById to find the <div> in the <body> of our page. Finally, we use innerHTML to get the contents of the <div>. Everything in our <div> will now be saved in localStorage.

We want to save our list every time an item is added or removed, so we also need to make sure the addItem and removeItem functions call the saveList function after they have run.

Loading the List

To load the list, we need to create a second function. Whenever the loadList function is called, it will set the innerHTML of the <div> with the id "list" to whatever has been saved in localStorage.

We need to call our loadList function so that when our browser finishes loading, it loads our list too. To make sure we don't try to load a list that hasn't been saved, we have to use an if statement before we try to use localStorage. The if statement we need looks like this:

```
<div id="list"></div>
<script>
  if(localStorage.storedList) {
    loadList();
  }
</script>
```

load list function call

The if statement checks whether there is a list saved in localStorage before trying to load it. When we save our complete code block and run our app in our browser, items we add to the list are now saved even if we close and then reopen our file.

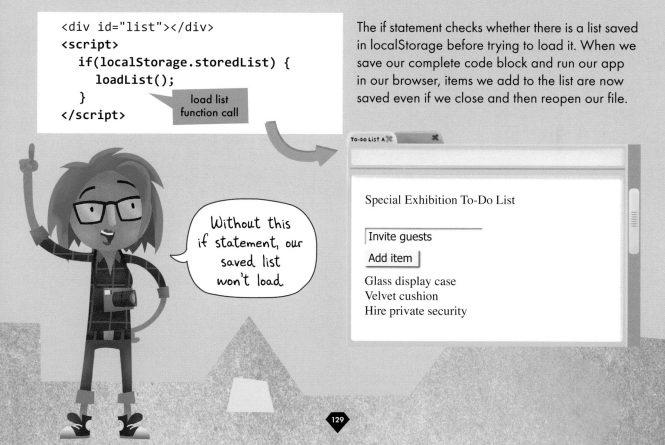

Without this if statement, our saved list won't load.

Removing Items from localStorage

There's just one more thing we have to do to make our loadList function work properly. At the moment, when you use the to-do list app, you'll be able to add or remove an item by clicking on it. But if you load your saved list from localStorage, you won't be able to remove an item when you click on it.

This is because we're only saving the HTML elements into localStorage, not the onclick attribute that we add when each element is created. We need to add the onclick attribute back to each of our list items, so that the removeItem function still works after we load our list from localStorage. We need to add one final piece of code to our loadList function in our `<head>`, so it looks like this:

```
function loadList() {
    document.getElementById("list").innerHTML = localStorage.storedList;
    for(var i = 0; i < list.children.length; i++) {
        list.children[i].onclick = removeItem;
    }
}
```

code that starts the loop

code to run in loop

condition for loop

We've now added a **loop** to our loadList function. This loop adds our onclick attribute to our removeItem function on every item that we load from localStorage. It counts up through each new HTML element that we've added to our to-do list and sets the onclick attribute for each new element.

You will learn more about loops in Mission 5, but for now you should know that loops are split into three parts.

CODE WORDS

A **LOOP** is a special piece of JavaScript that runs the same piece of code again and again. Programmers use loops so they don't have to type the same piece of code over and over.

A loop needs:

- The code that starts the loop
- The condition to check whether the loop is allowed to run
- Code that runs every time the loop runs

That's very clever coding!

DO-IT-YOURSELF TASK
BUILD A TO-DO LIST APP

Now use all the new skills you've learned in this mission to build the to-do list app Professor Bairstone needs for the Monk Diamond special exhibition. Use JavaScript with the DOM and localStorage APIs to make a to-do list that Professor Bairstone can add items to. Make sure that when he completes a task, he can click on the item to remove it from the list.

The TO-DO List App Brief

When you code your app, use HTML and JavaScript and the new APIs. Make sure you include these things:

● **A function that adds an item to the list using the DOM**

● **A function that removes an item from the list using the DOM**

● **A function that saves the list using localStorage**

● **A function that loads the list using localStorage**

● **A text box the user can type the items into**

● **A button that the user can click to add an item to the list**

Save your file in your **Coding** folder and call it **listapp.html**.

Turn the page to see the entire code block you need for your app!

Don't forget to use the Get Coding! website if you need help.

```
<!DOCTYPE html>
<html>
<head>
   <title>To-Do List App</title>
   <script>
     function addItem() {
        var newItem = document.createElement("div");
        newItem.innerHTML = document.getElementById("box").value;
        newItem.onclick = removeItem;
        document.getElementById("list").appendChild(newItem);
        saveList();
     }
     function removeItem() {
        document.getElementById("list").removeChild(this);
        saveList();
     }
     function saveList() {
        localStorage.storedList = document.getElementById("list").innerHTML;
     }
     function loadList() {
        document.getElementById("list").innerHTML = localStorage.storedList;
        for(var i = 0; i < list.children.length; i++) {
           list.children[i].onclick = removeItem;
        }
     }
   </script>
</head>
```

This special exhibition is going to be fantastic. I can't wait!

132

```
<body>
  <p>The House of Volkov</p>
  <p>Special Exhibition To-Do List</p>
  <br/>
  <input type="text" id="box" value="Type here to add task"/>
  <br/>
  <input type="button" value="Add item" onclick="addItem();"/>
  <br/>
  <div id="list"></div>
  <script>
    if(localStorage.storedList) {
      loadList();
    }
  </script>
</body>
</html>
```

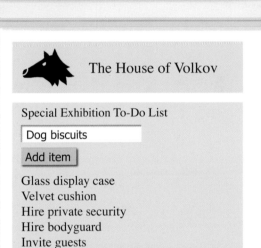

Now use CSS to change the design of your app so it looks like this!

FUTURE CODE SKILLS

Using APIs like the DOM and localStorage when you're coding with HTML, CSS, and JavaScript allows you to create more complex and interactive web pages or web-based apps. Now you can use the DOM to access some powerful features in your browser. It allows you to dynamically make changes to the HTML as your user interacts with your page or app. Great work!

PLAN A ROUTE

- **LEARN HOW TO ADD CONTENT FROM ANOTHER WEB PAGE**

- **EMBED A MAP IN YOUR PAGE USING A WEB API**

- **USE AN API KEY**

- **LEARN HOW THE ‹IFRAME› TAG WORKS**

- **PLAN A ROUTE USING GOOGLE MAPS**

Mission Brief

Dear Coder,

You will be pleased to hear that we have finally made it to Moscow after a long train journey. We are currently lying low at a secret location, as we want no one but Mr. Volkov to know we've arrived in the city with the Monk Diamond. Mr. Volkov came to see us — he's a charming man. I'm so happy we found his lost jewel

He and Professor Bairstone have been extremely busy getting everything ready for the exhibition. Your app has been very helpful, and so far everything is going according to plan. There is only one thing that Professor Bairstone and Mr. Volkov haven't thought of: How do we safely transport the diamond from our secret location to the House of Volkov?

The Bond Brothers have been known to ambush and rob courier vans transporting expensive jewelry in daring heists. I'm sending you an entry from the Explorer's Encyclopedia so you can see what I mean. We could deliver the diamond to the shop ourselves, but Professor Bairstone is such a famous figure that I'm worried we will draw attention to ourselves and therefore the exhibition plans.

We've decided that the best thing to do would be for me to take the diamond to Gorky Park. Mr. Volkov's head of security will be waiting for me, and together we will take the diamond to the House of Volkov, which is right next to St. Basil's Cathedral. Would you be able to help us by planning a route through the city? It will be really helpful to have a web page with a map embedded in it. It would be terrible if we got lost or were duped by the Bond Brothers into going the wrong way. Imagine if we lost the Monk Diamond now!

Thank you for helping us again. Everything is so nearly ready. We've just had the invitations for the exhibition printed and they are now ready to be sent to the guests. I'm sending you one too!

Very best wishes from our city hideaway,
Dr. Ruby Day

THE EXPLORER'S
ENCYCLOPEDIA
The Guide to Every Adventure

Home page
Contents
Featured discoveries
Famous explorers
Historical expeditions

The Bond Brothers' Robberies

From the Explorer's Encyclopedia: The Guide to Every Adventure

For other jewel thieves, see <u>Famous Jewel Thieves</u>.

The **Bond Brothers' Robberies** are the audacious jewel thefts carried out by the gang of <u>jewel thieves</u> known as the <u>Bond Brothers</u>. The majority of the <u>jewels</u> taken in their raids have never been seen again. Normally, stolen jewelry is sold on the <u>black market</u> soon after a theft, but the Bond Brothers are thought to have a top-secret hiding place for their loot.

*Mr. V. Volkov requests the pleasure
of your company*

*at a very special exhibition hosted by
the House of Volkov*

*on June 21 at 7:00 p.m. at
the House of Volkov, near
St. Basil's Cathedral, Moscow*

*You are invited to meet guests of honor
Professor Bairstone, Dr. Day,
and Ernest*

*and to hear about the sensational discovery
made on their recent expedition*

RSVP

Interpol knows that the gang has three core members, who are known only by their aliases: Light Fingers, Gemma the Gem, and Tony Twinkles. The three members are aided by lesser-known associates who help them choose their targets, make their escapes, and hide the stolen jewels.

One of the gang is a skilled cybercriminal, with access to government databases. In all their robberies, the CCTV cameras in the area surrounding the target are disabled during the period of the crime.

In addition to stealing from expensive boutiques in smash-and-grab raids, the Bond Brothers have held up courier vans and motorcycles delivering jewelry. They have disguised themselves as road workers and then used fake road signs to direct the drivers onto dead-end roads before robbing them.

Their success seems to be due to the way they vary their tactics. No raid is ever the same as another, making it very hard for the authorities to predict what they will do next.

ADDING CONTENT USING A WEB API

Now that you've read the Mission Brief and know what Dr. Day needs you to do, let's get coding! This will be a bit different from what you've done in the other three missions, but don't worry. The great thing about learning how to build web pages or apps that use the Internet is that you don't always have to do the hard work yourself.

It might sound like a challenge to create a web page with a map **embedded** in it, but we don't have to code the map from scratch. All we have to do is write some code to call a URL on the Internet that has the map we need. Programmers call this integrating one web page with another.

When we want to integrate our web page with another website, we have to write some code that will connect our page to the web server that stores the other website. We can then access the data and content that we need on that server.

Web APIS

You already know what an API is and have used two of them in Mission 3: the DOM and localStorage APIs. Those APIs let you access some handy built-in functions. APIs come in all shapes and sizes, and the API that we need to embed a map in this mission is slightly different from those we have used already.

APIs used to integrate with other websites are sometimes called web APIs or web services. They let you access a website's built-in features and functions, so you can add extra content to your page without having to write lots of code.

You can use web APIs for lots of different things when you're building a website. You might have come across some of these web APIs on websites, which help you do these things:

- **Add maps**
- **Add *Like* or *Share* buttons for Facebook**
- **Share videos on YouTube and Twitch**

4

Web APIs let everyone build better and more complex websites quickly and easily. To embed a map and plan a route, we are going to use a map web API.

There are several websites on the Internet that let you embed their maps on your web pages. Most of them even let you do it for free. The most popular free map web APIs are Google Maps and Bing Maps, which are run by Google and Microsoft.

We're going to learn how you can use Google Maps to find the best route for Dr. Day and the House of Volkov's head of security. You've probably used Google Maps before to look up an address, but this time you are going to learn how to program your very own map and then embed it in your web page.

Map Web APIS

To use the Google Maps web API, you have to register with Google and get a special piece of code called an API key. An API key is a special password that your web page uses to access the Google Maps API on the Google server. If you don't use an API key, you won't be able to embed a map. You can get a Google Maps API key by visiting:

```
https://developers.google.com/maps/documentation/embed/
```

An API key is a long piece of code made up of letters and numbers. Every one is different, but will look something like this:

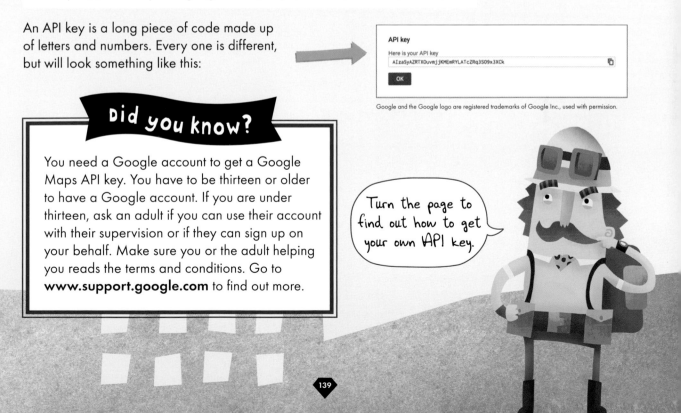

API key

Here is your API key

AIzaSyAZRTXOuvmjjKMEmRYLATcZRq3SO9x3XCk

OK

Google and the Google logo are registered trademarks of Google Inc., used with permission.

Did you know?

You need a Google account to get a Google Maps API key. You have to be thirteen or older to have a Google account. If you are under thirteen, ask an adult if you can use their account with their supervision or if they can sign up on your behalf. Make sure you or the adult helping you reads the terms and conditions. Go to **www.support.google.com** to find out more.

Turn the page to find out how to get your own API key.

CODE SKILLS ► GETTING A GOOGLE MAPS API KEY

Let's learn how you can get a Google Maps API key. You'll need it later in the mission to create the route for Dr. Day.

1. Start by going to the Google Maps API website. Type this link into your browser:

```
https://developers.google.com/maps/documentation/embed/
```

2. Find the *GET A KEY* button. Click on it.

3. You'll see a pop-up with three options. Click *CONTINUE*.

4. Now sign in to a Google account. Remember, if you are under thirteen, you need to get an adult to help you. You will be sent to the Google Developers Console. Make sure you (if you are over the age requirement) or the adult helping you reads the terms and conditions. You need to agree to them in order to proceed. Then select *Create a new project* from the drop-down list and click *Continue*.

5. You will then be asked to create an API key. Don't fill anything in – just click Create.

6. Your API key will be displayed. It will be a long code made up of numbers and letters. Each key is unique, but it will look a bit like this:

7. Now copy and paste your API key into your text-editing program. Save your file in your **Coding** folder as a text file (use the extension **.txt**). Call your new file **APIkey.txt**.

Keep your API key safe, because you'll need it later in the mission!

Coder, take note! Some of these steps might change as Google updates its software.

HOW TO EMBED CONTENT

Now that you know what embedding is and you've got an API key for Google Maps, we can start making our web page for Dr. Day. We first need to learn how to embed content from another website in our web page. To do this, we need to learn some new HTML tags and attributes.

The <iframe> Tag: <iframe> and </iframe>

To add a Google Map to our page, we need to use a new HTML tag called the <iframe> tag. The opening tag is <iframe> and the closing tag is </iframe>. The tag is used to create an inline frame, which is a really useful way of embedding content from another website in your page. You can also use several attributes with the tag to change the way your embedded content displays.

The first attribute you have to include is the source (src) attribute, which we used in Mission 1. The source attribute tells your browser which piece of content you want to embed and is in the form of a URL. When you are integrating your website, the information in the URL is very important for your browser. Let's take a look at an example with the Monk Diamond Discovery page:

```
<!DOCTYPE html>
<html>
<head>
    <title>Diamond Discovery</title>
</head>
<body>
                    source attribute
    <iframe src="https://www.monkdiamonddiscovery.com">
    </iframe>
</body>
</html>
```

<iframe>

URL

A small section of the Monk Diamond Discovery web page that we provided as a URL will appear embedded in your page. However, it's quite hard to see the embedded page at this small size. You need to include some other attributes inside your opening <iframe> tag to change the size, shape, and appearance of the embedded page. Let's look at all the attributes you can use:

Attribute name	What does it do?	Example values
src	Provides the URL for the piece of content you want to embed	http://www.bing.com
width	Sets the maximum width of the `<iframe>`	600px, 20%
height	Sets the maximum height of the `<iframe>`	600px, 20%
frameborder	Sets the width of the border around the `<iframe>`	0px, 4px
style	Sets the style of the `<iframe>` using a CSS property and value	border: 0px

Now let's see how we can use all these attributes to change the appearance of our `<iframe>` and embedded content. Remember, you always have to add attributes inside your opening tag, like this:

```
<!DOCTYPE html>
<html>
<head>
    <title>Diamond Discovery</title>
</head>
<body>
    <iframe
        width="350px"          width attribute
        height="350px"         frameborder attribute
        frameborder="0px"
        style="border: 0px"    style attribute
        src="https://www.monkdiamonddiscovery.com">
    </iframe>
</body>
</html>
```

height attribute

Useful thing, this `<iframe>` tag!

Here, we've set the width and height attributes to the same number of pixels to make our `<iframe>` into a square. The frameborder attribute and the CSS border property have both been set to 0 pixels. This is so the `<iframe>` will blend in to the page. You normally do this with an `<iframe>`, so that the embedded content looks like it is part of your page.

CODE SKILLS ► USING THE <IFRAME> TAG

Now that you've read about the <iframe> tag and how it works, let's try using the tag and its attributes to change the way a piece of embedded content displays in a web page.

1. Open up your text-editing program. Create a new HTML file called **iframe.html**. Add the opening and closing <iframe> tags to the <body> of your page, so the code in your new file looks like this:

```
<!DOCTYPE html>
<html>
<head>
   <title>iFrames</title>
</head>
<body>
   <iframe>
   </iframe>
</body>
</html>
```

2. Now set the attributes of your <iframe>. Include the width, height, frameborder, and style attributes inside your opening <iframe> tag, like this:

```
<body>
   <iframe
      width="350px"
      height="350px"
      frameborder="0px"
      style="border: 0px">
   </iframe>
</body>
```

3. Finally, add the source attribute. Set its value to the URL of a website, like this:

```
<iframe
   width="350px"
   height="350px"
   frameborder="0px"
   style="border: 0px"
   src="https://www.bing.com">
</iframe>
```

4. Save your HTML file and open it in your browser. Your chosen site will be embedded in your web page.
   Now try changing the height and width of your <iframe> and seeing what it does to the embedded content.

I really like this way of embedding new content in our page.

EMBEDDING A GOOGLE MAP

As you can see, the `<iframe>` tag is really useful. Let's learn now how we can integrate a Google Map into our page using it. The simplest kind of Google Map you can add is called an embedded search. You use a Google API called the Google Maps Embed API. When the user gives the API a keyword, such as the name of a country, city, or street, it will produce a map based on that keyword.

URLs

You need to provide the Google Maps Embed API with a URL in the source attribute of your `<iframe>`. The URL has to contain several important pieces of information for the correct map to be embedded. Let's see exactly what information we need to include in a URL if we want to embed a map of Moscow in our web page:

API key

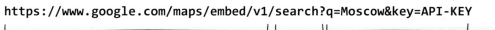

```
https://www.google.com/maps/embed/v1/search?q=Moscow&key=API-KEY
```

path   search API function   query string parameters

The first part of the URL is the path to the Google Maps Embed API. You then have to tell that API what built-in function you want to use. We want to use the search API function on the Google server, so we add that to the URL. The next piece of information is the specific part of our request, called the query **string parameters**.

 CODE WORDS

A **STRING** is a piece of data in the form of a sequence of characters. Strings can be made up of words and numbers.

A **PARAMETER** is another name for a piece of information, or an argument, that is passed to a function so it can perform an action.

String Parameters

The string parameters are the parts of a URL that contain variables — the pieces of information that depend on the user. In our example, there are two parameters. The two variables are the map we are searching for (Moscow) and our unique API key.

We have to structure our query string parameters in a certain way, so the Google server is able to access information stored in our variables. The two parts of the query string parameters are the key and the value. You need both of these parts for your parameters to work. Turn the page to see the URL for the map of Moscow.

```
https://www.google.com/maps/embed/v1/search?q=Moscow&key=API-KEY
```

key   value   key   value

In this URL, the two parameters are separated by an ampersand (&). The first is the query key and the second is the API key. Your browser needs them both because they contain this important information:

Parameter key	What does it do?	Example value
q	Gives the location you want to search for	Moscow, London
key	Gives the API key needed to access the Google server	API-KEY

The Google Maps Embed API needs these two parameters to find the map we want to embed and then to integrate it into our page. Let's see what happens if we use these two parameters in our URL and set it as the source attribute for our `<iframe>`. When we save our file and open it in our browser, we will see a map of Moscow embedded in our page.

```
<!DOCTYPE html>
<html>
<head>
    <title>Moscow</title>
</head>
<body>
    <iframe
        width="450px"
        height="450px"
        frameborder="0px"
        style="border: 0px"
        src="https://www.google.com/maps/embed/v1/search?q=Moscow&key=API-KEY">
    </iframe>
</body>
</html>
```

CODE SKILLS ► EMBED A GOOGLE MAP

Let's embed a Google Map for Moscow in a page. It's an important skill to master before we plan our route for Dr. Day and the head of security.

1. Open up your text-editing program. Create a new HTML file called **citymap.html**. Then copy and paste your code from **iframe.html** into your new file. Modify it so that it looks like this:

```
<!DOCTYPE html>
<html>
<head>
    <title>City Map</title>
</head>
<body>
    <iframe>
    </iframe>
</body>
</html>
```

2. Now add the width, height, frameborder, and style attributes inside your opening `<iframe>` tag. Set the values, like this:

```
<body>
    <iframe
        width="450px"
        height="450px"
        frameborder="0px"
        style="border: 0px">
    </iframe>
</body>
```

3. Add the source attribute inside your opening `<iframe>` tag. Use the Google Maps Embed API URL and add the two parameters. Set the parameter "q" to the location you want for your map and the parameter "key" to the unique API key that you got earlier in the mission. Your source attribute will look like this:

```
<iframe
    width="450px"
    height="450px"
    frameborder="0px"
    style="border: 0px"
    src="https://www.google.com/maps/embed/
        v1/search?q=Moscow&key=API-KEY">
</iframe>
```

4. Save your HTML file and open it in your browser. You will see your map embedded in your page.

PLAN A ROUTE USING GOOGLE MAPS

Now that you know how to embed a map in your page, we can start planning the route Dr. Day and the head of security need to take through Moscow. To do this, we need to build a new URL and use a new function in the Google Maps Embed API. We have to create our URL in a slightly different way.

We need to use the directions function, rather than the search function. The directions function will create a map that gives a route from a specified location to another specified location. Dr. Day needs to take the Monk Diamond from Gorky Park to St. Basil's Cathedral, so our new URL will look like this:

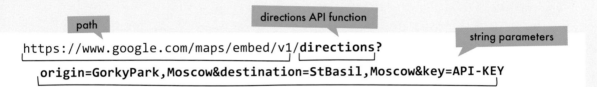

path

directions API function

string parameters

```
https://www.google.com/maps/embed/v1/directions?
origin=GorkyPark,Moscow&destination=StBasil,Moscow&key=API-KEY
```

Like before, the first part of our URL is the path to the Google Maps Embed API. We then request to use the directions API function. Then we use three parameters: the origin, destination, and API key. For the origin and destination, you can put lots of different values, but the simplest thing to do is put the place name followed by the city name. These two new keys are important for your browser, because they provide the following information:

Parameter key	What does it do?	Example value
origin	Gives the place you want your route to start	GorkyPark,Moscow
destination	Gives the place you want your route to end	StBasil,Moscow

Did you notice?

We've included the name of the site and the city, separated by a comma (,). There is no space after the comma.

I can't wait to see St. Basil's Cathedral!

Let's add our new URL to our source attribute and see the route Dr. Day and the head of security need to take through Moscow:

```
<!DOCTYPE html>
<html>
<head>
  <title>Top-Secret Route</title>
</head>
<body>
  <iframe
    width="650px"
    height="650px"
    frameborder="0px"
    style="border: 0px"
    src="https://www.google.com/maps/embed/v1/directions?
      origin=GorkyPark,Moscow&destination=StBasil,Moscow&key=
      API-KEY">
  </iframe>
</body>
</html>
```

> This is exactly what Dr. Day needs to get the Monk Diamond safely to the House of Volkov!

DO-IT-YOURSELF TASK
PLAN A ROUTE

Great work! You've learned how to use a web API and Google Maps to embed content in your page. Now use your new knowledge to plan a route through Moscow, from Gorky Park to St. Basil's Cathedral. Having a route will help Dr. Day keep the Monk Diamond safe.

Moscow Route Planning Brief

When you plan your route, use your new Code Skills to do the following things:

- **Use an API key**: use the Google Maps Embed API to get an API key.

- **Create an `<iframe>`**: use this new HTML tag so you can embed content in your page.

- **Change the way your `<iframe>` displays**: use attributes to change the height, width, and borders of your `<iframe>`.

- **Use the source attribute**: embed a URL that will connect to the web API you need.

- **Use the Google Maps Embed API**: create a Google Map using the Google API.

- **Use the built-in direction function**: plot a route using this function.

- **Set query string parameters**: give the destination function the origin and destination for your route.

Save your file in your **Coding** folder and call it **route.html**.

```
<!DOCTYPE html>
<html>
<head>
  <title>Top-Secret Route</title>
</head>
<body>
  <iframe
    width="1000px"
    height="1000px"
    frameborder="0px"
    style="border: 0px"
    src="https://www.google.com/maps/embed/v1/directions?
       origin=GorkyPark,Moscow&destination=StBasil,Moscow&key=API-KEY">
  </iframe>
</body>
</html>
```

Don't forget to use your saved API key.

FUTURE CODE SKILLS

Knowing how to use web APIs means you can easily include features from other apps or websites in your code. You can use them to build pages and apps that use big web services, such as social networks like Facebook or Instagram, or utilities like Google Maps or Dropbox. This will save you time and keep you from having to code functions from scratch.

This is what your finished code will look like!

This route will stop the Bond Brothers and keep the Monk Diamond safe!

MAKE A GAME

- **USE TIMERS IN JAVASCRIPT**

- **LEARN WHAT GAME LOOPS ARE AND HOW THEY WORK**

- **LEARN HOW TO ANIMATE HTML ELEMENTS WITH JAVASCRIPT**

- **BUILD A GAME THAT TESTS REACTION TIMES**

Dear Coder,

The Monk Diamond arrived at the House of Volkov yesterday. Dr. Day and I are both so grateful for your help with planning the route. All seemed to go smoothly, although Dr. Day did think a bearded man wearing a large hat might have been following them. He vanished quickly, but she was slightly alarmed. Thank goodness the diamond arrived safely.

It's been positioned in its new glass case, on its new cushion, and it looks dazzling! We've just been arranging the snacks on silver platters, which was the final task on our list. Everything is now ready for the grand opening of the exhibition tonight.

Between you and me, ever since the incident with the boulder, I have been worried about our security arrangements. I know we have been very careful to keep the discovery of the Monk Diamond a secret, and you did a great job creating a password for our web page. But I am worried that the Bond Brothers might still be on our trail (don't forget we think one of them is a skilled cybercriminal). My biggest fear is that they could sabotage the exhibition by stealing the diamond again.

An old pal in London who works for one of the city's most famous museums recently told me she has trained a superb new security team using a computer game. I didn't believe her until she showed me the data. The game sharpened the team's reaction times significantly, and they responded to suspicious circumstances at the museum far more quickly than they had before they played the game.

I was wondering if you could help me by building a game that will test the reaction times of the House of Volkov's security team. I'm tied up this afternoon, as I still need to buy Ernest a new collar, so I was really hoping you could help. I've attached one of my private entries on the Explorer's Encyclopedia. It contains sensitive information about the exhibition, so please don't share it with anyone.

Thank you again for your excellent help. Warmest wishes from bustling Moscow, Professor Harry Bairstone

The House of Volkov's Security Team

From the Explorer's Encyclopedia: The Guide to Every Adventure

Home page
Contents
Featured discoveries
Famous explorers
Historical expeditions

This is a private entry with restricted access. To view the public entry for the House of Volkov, click <u>here</u>.

The **House of Volkov's Security Team** protects the highly valuable <u>jewels</u> on display in the <u>House of Volkov's private collection</u>. Since the theft of the <u>Monk Diamond</u>, the jewels on display in the store are kept in locked cases made of reinforced glass that is two hundred times stronger than normal glass.

The Security Training Game Rules

- ◆ Every second, 6 people will be shown on-screen.

- ◆ 5 will be guests; 1 will be a thief.

- ◆ If you click on the thief, you gain 1 point.

- ◆ If you click on a guest, you lose 2 points.

- ◆ This happens 6 times in total.

- ◆ The aim of the game is to spot all 6 thieves and score 6 points.

In light of the theft, the owner, Viktor Volkov, has trained his security team to be on the alert for any customers behaving suspiciously. In the last year, several petty crooks have been caught trying to unlock the display cases with skeleton keys.

The special exhibition Mr. Volkov is hosting for the Monk Diamond will be the most high-profile event ever held by the House of Volkov. Mr. Volkov decided to consult Professor Harry Bairstone about the security strategy for the opening night of the exhibition.

The Bond Brothers have used disguises in past robberies and Mr. Volkov and Professor Bairstone are worried that members of the gang, or their associates, might try to infiltrate the exhibition by posing as guests.

The agreed-upon strategy is to use the method developed for museums in London by Professor Amy Li. A computer game with a simple set of rules has proved to be an effective way of sharpening the reaction times of members of a security team. The game needs to be built as soon as possible so that the team is properly trained before the opening of the special exhibition.

BUILDING A GAME

Now that you've read the brief for Mission 5, you're ready to start building your game. This mission works in a slightly different way from the missions you have completed so far. You are going to build the game as you work through the mission. Follow the step-by-step instructions and copy the code, and you'll have the game ready for Professor Bairstone in no time.

> It's going to be a rush to get the game built in time, so start coding quickly!

1. Create an HTML file

Just like in all the other missions, the first thing we need to do is create a new HTML file. Call your new HTML file **securitygame.html**. Copy this code into your text-editing program:

 Save your HTML file in your **Coding** folder on your desktop.

```
<!DOCTYPE html>
<html>
<head>
    <title>Security Game</title>
</head>
<body>
</body>
</html>
```

2. Build the game board

Now we need to build the basic structure of our game. We need to code a game board in our web page. The game board will be the area in our browser where the game will work. When the security team plays the game, the guests and thief will appear on the game board.

Add your game board by coding an empty `<div>` in the `<body>` of your page. Add an id attribute to your `<div>`. Your `<body>` code will look like this:

```
<body>
    <div id="board">
    </div>
</body>
```

id attribute

Then in your <head> add a CSS class that will change the look of your <div>. Use a CSS selector, called the id selector, to find your <div> by its id attribute. CSS selectors are an easy way to select various groups of elements to style. Using the CSS id selector is simple. All you have to do is create a class name using a hash (#) and the id attribute of the HTML element you want to change.

Create a CSS class called board that sets the CSS properties and values of your <div> to these things. The code for the CSS class in your <head> needs to look like this:

The game board needs:

- ♥ A 1px solid black border
- ♥ A gray background
- ♥ A height of 350px
- ♥ A width of 650px

> This is like the CSS element selector in Mission 1 or the CSS type attribute selector in Mission 3.

```
<head>
    <title>Security Game</title>
    <style>
      #board {
          border: 1px solid black;
          background-color: gray;
          height: 350px;
          width: 650px;
      }
    </style>
</head>
```

CSS id selector

Save your HTML file and open it in your browser. You will see your empty game board displayed on-screen.

Security Ga

> Great work!

3. Add a button

Now that we have a game board, we should add a button to our page. When the player clicks the button, the code for our game will run, and the game will start.

   Add your button above the `<div>` in your `<body>`. Create the button as you did in Mission 3, using the `<input/>` tag and type and value attributes. Set the onclick attribute of your `<input/>` tag to call a JavaScript function called startGame that will start the game. The code for your button will look like this:

```
<input type="button" value="Play" onclick="startGame()";/>
```

Now create the startGame function that your button will call when it's clicked. Add the function underneath the `<div>` in your `<body>`. Your `<script>` block will look like this:

```
<script>
  function startGame() {
  }
</script>
```

The complete code block in your text-editing program will now look like this:

```
<!DOCTYPE html>
<html>
<head>
   <title>Security Game</title>
   <style>
     #board {
        border: 1px solid black;
        background-color: gray;
        height: 350px;
        width: 650px;
     }
   </style>
</head>
<body>
   <input type="button" value="Play" onclick="startGame()";/>
   <div id="board">
   </div>
   <script>
     function startGame() {
     }
   </script>
</body>
</html>
```

button

function call

JavaScript function

You're becoming a real coding whiz!

Save your code and open it in your browser. You will see your button on-screen. At the moment, when you click it, nothing will happen. We need to add some code to our startGame function.

Let's get that button working!

4. Create a JavaScript timer

Our game is going to test the reaction times of the security team at the House of Volkov. For our game to work, we need to learn how we can use JavaScript to run a piece of code again and again, after a certain period of time has passed. This is called a timer.

JavaScript has a built-in timer function called setTimeout, which allows you to call a function after a given amount of time has passed. All you have to do is give the setTimeout function the name of the function you want to call and the amount of time as arguments. As you know from Mission 2, you pass a function an argument by putting the argument in parentheses. This time we are passing the function two arguments. Let's look at how you would use setTimeout to call a function after a certain time.

In this example, the gameTimer function will be called after 1 second, or 1,000 milliseconds.

setTimeout function

function to call

amount of time to call it after

```
setTimeout(gameTimer, 1000);
```

Did you notice?

You have to use milliseconds with the setTimeout function. There are 1,000 milliseconds in a second. To work out the number of milliseconds you need, multiply the number of seconds by 1,000. So if you wanted your function to be called after 3 seconds, you would multiply 3 by 1,000.

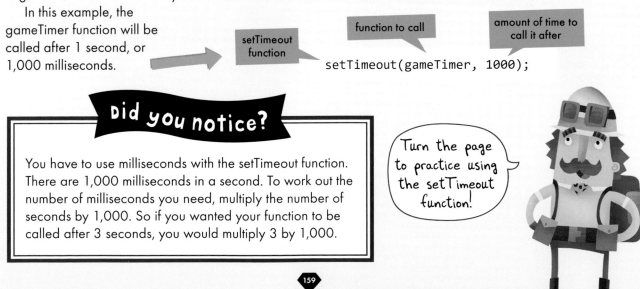

Turn the page to practice using the setTimeout function!

JavaScript timers, such as the setTimeout function, are very useful for building games. Let's try using the setTimeout function, so you know how it works and can add it to your game later in the mission. Let's code a program that counts up a number every second.

1. Open up your text-editing program. Create a new HTML file called **timers.html**. Type out this code:

```html
<!DOCTYPE html>
<html>
<head>
    <title>Timers</title>
</head>
<body>
    <div id="number">
    </div>
</body>
</html>
```

2. Now add the `<script>` tag to your `<head>`. Inside your `<script>` block, create a variable and set its value to 0 using the assignment (=) operator, like this:

```html
<head>
    <title>Timers</title>
    <script>
      var count = 0;
    </script>
</head>
```

3. Now create a function called updateCount. Every time the function is called, it will use the addition operator (+) to add 1 to the value of your variable. Then use getElementById and innerHTML to find your empty `<div>` and set the contents to the variable. Your code will look like this:

```html
<script>
    var count = 0;
    function updateCount() {
      count = count + 1;            [add 1]
      document.getElementById("number").innerHTML = count;
    }
</script>
```
[update screen]
[find <div>]

4. Now we need to add a function call to our `<body>`. Add the function call like this:

```
<body>
  <div id="number">
  </div>
    <script>
      updateCount();
    </script>
</body>
```

5. Finally, we have to add a timer that will call our function every second to our `<script>` block. We need to use the setTimeout function. We have to pass the function name and the number of milliseconds to the setTimeout function as arguments. Our `<script>` block will look like this:

```
<script>
  var count = 0;
  function updateCount() {
    count = count + 1;
    document.getElementById("number").innerHTML = count;
    setTimeout(updateCount, 1000);
  }
</script>
```

call updateCount in 1 second

Save your HTML file and open it in your browser. You will see your timer in action. The setTimeout function will call your updateCount function every second. The function will run, and every second, 1 will be added to the value of your variable. The number in your browser will update automatically.

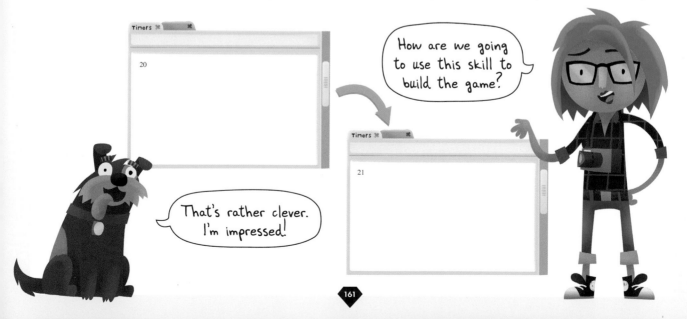

Tiners
20

How are we going to use this skill to build the game?

Tiners
21

That's rather clever. I'm impressed!

5. create a game loop

Games are one of the most difficult things you can code, and there are many different ways you can build them. A popular way is to use a game loop. You used a loop in Mission 3, and we are going to need to learn more about them to build our game.

A game loop is a JavaScript function that gets called over and over again while your game is running. You can use a game loop to check whether a player has done something, to draw an HTML element on your screen, and to run the code for the game.

We can use the setTimeout built-in function to create a game loop. We need to add a new function to our `<script>` block that pops up an alert every 3 seconds. Let's call this function gameLoop. This new function will be called when our button is clicked. Let's look at our code block:

```
<!DOCTYPE html>
<html>
<head>
    <title>Security Game</title>
    <style>
      #board {
        border: 1px solid black;
        background-color: gray;
        height: 350px;
        width: 650px;
      }
    </style>
</head>
<body>
    <input type="button" value="Play" onclick="startGame()";/>
    <div id="board">
    </div>
    <script>
    function startGame() {
        gameLoop();        ◄── function call
    }
    function gameLoop() {
        alert("Game over!");     ◄── alert
        setTimeout(gameLoop, 3000);
    }
    </script>
</body>
</html>
```

function

timer

number of milliseconds

> I wonder if I could sniff out the Bond Brothers. I've got a very good nose.

162

5

Once you have made these changes, save your code and open it in your browser. When you click your button and call your startGame function, the game loop will start to run. Your gameLoop function will be called every 3 seconds, and every time, an alert will pop up. Every time it pops up, press OK so it keeps popping up.

Great start to the mission! But where's the thief?

6. Add the guests and thief to the game board

Now that you've coded your game board, button, and game loop, we need to add the characters to our game. We want six different characters to flash on-screen in different places every second. Five of the characters will be guests; one character will be a thief. The security team will test their reaction times by trying to click on the thief when he or she flashes on-screen.

Let's start creating the characters on our game board. Each character needs its own `<div>`. Create six `<div>` tags nested inside your game board `<div>` and number them 1 to 6, like this:

Let's get these characters coded!

```
<div id="board">
    <div>1</div>
    <div>2</div>
    <div>3</div>
    <div>4</div>
    <div>5</div>
    <div>6</div>
</div>
```

Save your code and refresh your page. You will see your six <div> tags on your game board, like this:

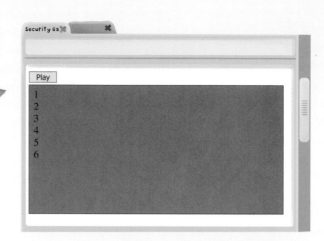

Now let's use CSS to change the design and layout of our <div> tags. Let's create a CSS class called character that will make our <div> tags square blue boxes. In your text-editing program, add this new CSS class to the <style> tag in your <head>. Your complete <style> block will now look like this:

```
<!DOCTYPE html>
<html>
<head>
    <title>Security Game</title>
    <style>
      #board {
        border: 1px solid black;
        background-color: gray;
        height: 350px;
        width: 650px;
      }
      .character {
        background-color: lightblue;
        width: 120px;
        height: 120px;
        padding: 10px;
        margin: 10px;
        float: left;
      }
    </style>
</head>
```

new CSS class

Did you notice?

We have used the float CSS property. This will make our <div> tags align with one another.

Then apply your new character CSS class to each of your six <div> tags using the class attribute, as you did in Mission 1. Your <body> will look like this:

```
<body>
   <input type="button" value="Play" onclick="startGame()";/>
   <div id="board">
      <div class="character">1</div>
      <div class="character">2</div>
      <div class="character">3</div>
      <div class="character">4</div>
      <div class="character">5</div>
      <div class="character">6</div>
   </div>
   <script>
      function startGame() {
         gameLoop();
      }
      function gameLoop() {
         alert("Game over!");
         setTimeout(gameLoop, 3000);
      }
   </script>
</body>
</html>
```

class attribute

It's starting to look more like a game now!

Save your code and refresh your page.
You will see the CSS properties applied to your <div> tags.

Something's making my nose itch.

Security Ga

Play

| 1 | 2 | 3 | 4 |

| 5 | 6 |

7. Use the game loop to stop the game

Now that we've added our characters to the game board, we need to make some changes to our game loop. At the moment, it pops up an alert every 3 seconds. We need to change our loop so it will stop after a certain period of time. We're going to do this by counting how many times we loop. When our loop has run a certain number of times, our game will end.

To count our loops, let's create a variable that will increase in value every time it's called. To do that, we should code a variable called loops that is set to the value 0. Add this variable to your <script> block before your gameLoop function, like this:

```
<script>
  function startGame() {
    gameLoop();
  }                     variable
  var loops = 0;
  function gameLoop() {
    alert("Game over!");
    setTimeout(gameLoop, 3000);
  }
</script>
```

We need to use this variable in our gameLoop function. We want to add 1 to its value every time the function is called. To do this, we could code like this:

```
loops = loops + 1;
```

However, we can actually use a new JavaScript operator to write the same instruction in a simpler and shorter way. It's called the increment operator (++), and it's just like the operators we learned about in Mission 2. We can use the increment operator (++) to add 1 to the value of our variable. All we have to write is this:

```
                        increment
                        operator
loops++;
```

We can use the increment operator (++) in our gameLoop function to count how many times our loop has been called. Remove the alert from your gameLoop function and replace it with your new piece of code, like this:

```
function gameLoop() {
  loops++;
  setTimeout(gameLoop, 3000);
}
```

This gives me paws for thought!

166

Now we want to make sure that our game loops for a fixed number of times before the game ends. We do this by adding an if statement and an else statement to our gameLoop function, which will keep track of how many times our loop has run.

We need to make sure that when the loop has run for a certain number of times, the setTimeout function calling the loop will stop and an alert will pop up. We want our loop to run 12 times. It will run every 3 seconds until the twelfth loop, when the game will end. Our game will last for a total of 33 seconds (11 multiplied by 3) before it ends on the twelfth loop. Let's look at our whole <script> block with the new variable, if statement, and else statement:

```
<script>
  function startGame() {
    gameLoop();
  }
  var loops = 0;
  function gameLoop() {
    loops++;
    if(loops < 12) {          timer
      setTimeout(gameLoop, 3000);
    }
    else {
      alert("Game over!");
    }
  }
</script>
```

if statement

else statement

The if statement keeps track of how many times our loop has run. If it is less than (<) 12 times, it keeps running by calling setTimeout again. If it is 12 times or more, the else statement runs and an alert pops up.

 Save your new code and refresh your page. Press the *Play* button and wait until the alert pops up. Your game will now end after a certain period of time.

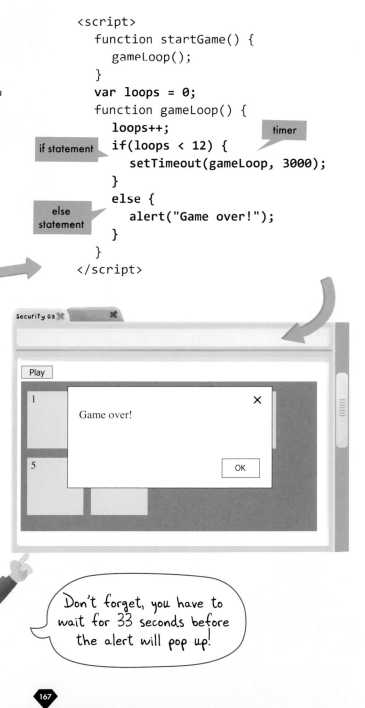

Don't forget, you have to wait for 33 seconds before the alert will pop up!

8. Use CSS to show and hide the characters

During our game, the guest and thief characters will flash on-screen. The House of Volkov security team will have to spot and click on the thief before he or she disappears. We need to use CSS to make the characters appear and disappear as the game loop runs. To do this, we have to learn a new CSS property that makes an HTML element appear or disappear from our browser. We can then use JavaScript to apply the property to our characters.

CSS property name	What does it do?	Example values
display	Changes how an HTML element appears on-screen	block, none

The display CSS property has lots of different values. The two values we need for our game are "block" and "none". If you set the display property of an HTML element to none, the element will not appear on your screen. If you set the display property to block, the HTML element will display as a square.

In your text-editing program, add two new CSS classes called hidden and visible. Use the display property so your `<style>` block looks like this:

 Save your code.

Let's try using this new CSS property!

```
<style>
  #board {
    border: 1px solid black;
    background-color: gray;
    height: 350px;
    width: 650px;
  }
  .character {
    background-color: lightblue;
    width: 120px;
    height: 120px;
    padding: 10px;
    margin: 10px;
    float: left;
  }
  .hidden {
    display: none;
  }
  .visible {
    display: block;
  }
</style>
```

display CSS property

CODE SKILLS ►USING THE DISPLAY CSS PROPERTY

Try using the CSS display property to make HTML elements appear and disappear on your screen. You'll need this to make your characters display correctly in your game.

1. Open up your text-editing program. Create a new HTML file called **display.html**. Type out the code below, then save your HTML file and open it in your browser. Your page will look like this:

```html
<!DOCTYPE html>
<html>
<head>
    <title>Display</title>
</head>
<body>
    <div>Security</div>
    <div>Thief</div>
    <div>Guest</div>
</body>
</html>
```

Display

Security
Thief
Guest

2. Reopen your file in your text-editing program. Modify your second `<div>` by adding the display CSS property so it looks like this:

```html
<body>
    <div>Security</div>
    <div style="display: none;">Thief</div>
    <div>Guest</div>
</body>
```

3. Save your file and refresh your page. The display CSS property and none value will make your second `<div>` disappear from your screen.

Display

Security
Guest

Where did that element go?

9. Animate the characters

We now need to apply our two new CSS classes (hidden and visible) to our game loop so the character `<div>` tags become animated. To do this, we need our game loop to add and remove the new CSS classes to and from our character `<div>` tags.

When our game runs, we want our characters to flash on and off the screen. We're currently looping around 12 times, so the character `<div>` tags need to be visible for 6 loops and invisible for 6 loops to create the flashing effect. The first thing we need is a new variable called peopleVisible to store this information. We need to set this variable to the value false, like this:

```
var peopleVisible = false
```

We need our variable to be set to false at the start so that the character `<div>` tags start off hidden on our screen. Then when the variable is set to true, the characters will appear on our screen.

When the game loop runs, we want the value stored in our new variable to alternate between true and false. To do this, we have to use another JavaScript operator, called the not operator (!). You can use the not operator (!) to change the value of your variable.

Let's look at how we use the not operator (!) in our `<script>` block. Type these new pieces of code into your text-editing program and save your file.

```
<script>
  function startGame() {
    gameLoop();
  }
  var loops = 0;              variable
  var peopleVisible = false;
  function gameLoop() {
    peopleVisible = !peopleVisible;
    loops++;                  not operator
    if(loops < 12) {
      setTimeout(gameLoop, 3000);
    }
    else {
      alert("Game over!");
    }
  }
</script>
```

We have used the not operator (!) to alternate the value of our new variable. If the value of our variable is false, when the variable runs in our gameLoop function, the not operator (!) will change its value to true. And if the value of our variable is true, when the variable runs, the not operator (!) will change its value to false.

Every time our loop runs, the loops variable will go up by one and the peopleVisible variable will alternate between true and false. As we loop around, our variables will look like this:

Now we need to add a new function called flashCharacters to our `<script>` block that will make our character `<div>` tags appear on-screen when the variable value is true. We do this using our two new CSS classes. When the value is true, we want to use the visible CSS class, and when the value is false, we want to use the hidden CSS class. Turn the page to find out exactly how to code this flashCharacters function.

Loop number	Variable value
1	True
2	False
3	True
4	False
5	True
6	False
7	True
8	False
9	True
10	False
11	True
12	False
Game over	

I like using loops!

This new function sounds complicated!

10. Apply CSS using JavaScript

We need a new function that will apply a CSS class to the character `<div>` tags depending on the value of our variable. We should call this function flashCharacters. The function must find our game board, using getElementById, and store it in a variable called board. Then the function needs to pick a CSS class to apply to the character `<div>` tags. This will depend on the value of our peopleVisible variable.

To decide the CSS classes, we create a second variable called classToSet that will store the two names of the CSS classes we need to set. We choose the CSS classes using an if and else statement. We set the value of our classToSet variable to an **empty string**. This empty string is filled as the if and else statements run. If our peopleVisible variable is true, our classToSet variable will be set to the visible CSS class. If our peopleVisible variable is false, the else statement will change our classToSet variable to the hidden CSS class.

We then need to code a loop that counts the 6 character `<div>` tags. As the loop counts the `<div>` tags, it assigns the value of our classToSet variable to each `<div>`. We do this using the className method. The className method lets you set a CSS class on an HTML element in JavaScript.

Our complete function now looks like this:

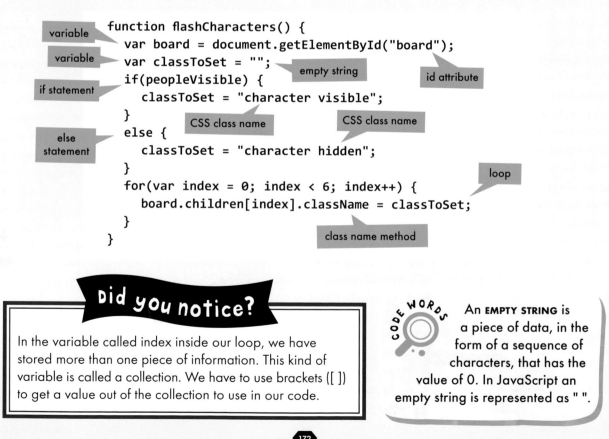

```javascript
function flashCharacters() {
    var board = document.getElementById("board");
    var classToSet = "";
    if(peopleVisible) {
        classToSet = "character visible";
    }
    else {
        classToSet = "character hidden";
    }
    for(var index = 0; index < 6; index++) {
        board.children[index].className = classToSet;
    }
}
```

variable
variable
if statement
else statement
empty string
id attribute
CSS class name
CSS class name
loop
class name method

Did you notice?

In the variable called index inside our loop, we have stored more than one piece of information. This kind of variable is called a collection. We have to use brackets ([ ]) to get a value out of the collection to use in our code.

CODE WORDS An **EMPTY STRING** is a piece of data, in the form of a sequence of characters, that has the value of 0. In JavaScript an empty string is represented as " ".

11. Simplify the conditional statements

This function looks quite complicated, so we should now try to simplify it. You can use another operator in JavaScript, called a conditional operator (?), to simplify the if and else statements. You use the conditional operator (?) like this:

conditional operator

```
var variableName = condition ? value1 : value2;
```

This tells our browser that if the condition of our variable is true, it should use value1, and if it is false, it should use value2. So we can rewrite the code in our function like this:

conditional operator   CSS class name   CSS class name

```
var classToSet = peopleVisible ? "character visible" : "character hidden";
```

Add your new flashCharacters function with the simplified if and else statements to your `<script>` block. Make sure your gameLoop function calls your new function too. Save your code and open it in your browser. Every 3 seconds, your blue boxes will appear and disappear on your screen.

Turn the page to see what our whole code block looks like now!

Get Coding!

Don't forget that you can view the code on the *Get Coding!* website too!

Check your code in your text-editing program. The code you need for your game will look like the block below. You have to refresh your page between each play of the game. Make any changes you need, and save your file.

```html
<!DOCTYPE html>
<html>
<head>
  <title>Security Game</title>
  <style>
    #board {
        border: 1px solid black;
        background-color: gray;
        height: 350px;
        width: 650px;
    }
    .character {
        background-color: lightblue;
        width: 120px;
        height: 120px;
        padding: 10px;
        margin: 10px;
        float: left;
    }
    .hidden {
        display: none;
    }
    .visible {
        display: block;
    }
  </style>
</head>
```

```html
<body>
  <input type="button" value="Play" onclick="startGame()";/>
  <div id="board">
    <div class="character">1</div>
    <div class="character">2</div>
    <div class="character">3</div>
    <div class="character">4</div>
    <div class="character">5</div>
    <div class="character">6</div>
  </div>
  <script>
    function startGame() {
      gameLoop();
    }
    var loops = 0;
    var peopleVisible = false;
    function gameLoop() {
      peopleVisible = !peopleVisible;
      flashCharacters();
      loops++;
      if(loops < 12) {
        setTimeout(gameLoop, 3000);
      }
      else {
        alert("Game over!");
      }
    }
    function flashCharacters() {
      var board = document.getElementById("board");
      var classToSet = peopleVisible ? "character visible" : "character hidden";
      for(var index = 0; index < 6; index++) {
        board.children[index].className = classToSet;
      }
    }
  </script>
</body>
</html>
```

function call

simplified if statement

But which characters are the guests and which is the thief?

Turn the page to create the characters!

175

12. create the thief

At the moment in our game, every 3 seconds, our characters flash on and off the screen. What we need to do now is change the position of our characters on-screen every time our game loop runs. Every 3 seconds, the characters need to move to a different place on the game board. And we need to make one of the characters the thief.

We first need to add a function that creates a new set of characters, in different positions, every time our game loop runs. Let's call this function createCharacters. Start by adding the function call in your gameLoop function, like this:

```
function gameLoop() {
  peopleVisible = !peopleVisible;
  createCharacters();
  flashCharacters();
  loops++;
  if(loops < 12) {
    setTimeout(gameLoop, 3000);
  }
  else {
    alert("Game over!");
  }
}
```

function call

Then code the new createCharacters function before your flashCharacters function:

```
function createCharacters() {
  var board = document.getElementById("board");
  for(var index = 0; index < 6; index ++) {
    board.children[index].innerHTML = "Guest";
  }
}
```

This is very similar to the function we coded earlier to set the CSS class of each character <div>. But this time we've used innerHTML, as we did in Mission 3, to set the value of each of the characters to "Guest".

Save your HTML file and refresh your page. Now when you click *Play*, you'll see that each of the character <div> tags is labeled "Guest".

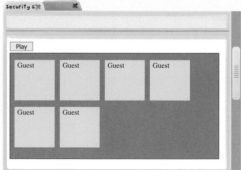

Now we need to add some code to our createCharacters function that will randomly pick one of the 6 character <div> tags to be the thief every time the game loop runs. We need to write code that will pick a random number. There isn't an easy way of picking a random number using JavaScript, so the next piece of code you need is quite complicated. Carefully type this new code at the end of your createCharacters function, so that it looks like this:

```
function createCharacters() {
  var board = document.getElementById("board");
  for(var index - 0; index < 6; index ++) {
      board.children[index].innerHTML = "Guest";
  }                           Math API
  var randomNumber = Math.floor(Math.random() * 6) + 1;
  board.children[randomNumber-1].innerHTML = "Thief";
}
```

Here, we are using a new API called the Math API. It works in exactly the same way as the DOM and localStorage APIs that we used in Mission 3. Using the Math API lets you access handy math functions that have been built in to your web browser. To find a random number, you have to do the following calculation:

```
Math.floor(Math.random() * BIGGEST_NUMBER) + SMALLEST_NUMBER;
```

We have 6 characters in our game, so our biggest number is 6 and our smallest number is 1. We need to code:

```
Math.floor(Math.random() * 6) + 1;
```

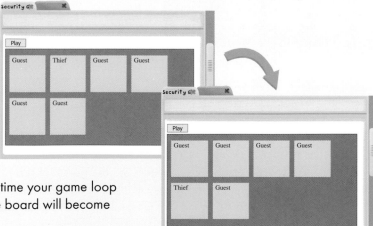

We must get the diamond back!

We then store the result of our calculation in a variable. Then we can use this variable in our next line of code. We use innerHTML to set the value of whichever <div> matches our random number, like this:

```
board.children[randomNumber-1].innerHTML = "Thief"
```

Because our numbers in JavaScript count up from 0, we're going to subtract 1 from our random number, so we'll only ever get the numbers 0, 1, 2, 3, 4, and 5.

 Save your code. Your new createCharacter function will have added a thief to your game. Now when you click *Play*, every time your game loop runs, a random character on your game board will become the thief.

13. Create a Score

Now we have a game board that shows us a different set of characters every 3 seconds. One of those characters is the thief that the House of Volkov's security team needs to catch. What we need to do now is create a way for the user to click on the thief. When the user clicks, they catch the thief and score a point.

We first have to add a variable called gameScore to keep track of the score. It goes underneath the startGame function at the top of our `<script>` block:

```
var loops = 0;
var peopleVisible = false;
var gameScore = 0;
```

Every time the player clicks on the thief, we need to add 1 point to their score. And to make sure the player is paying attention, every time they click on a guest, we should take away 2 points. To create our scoring system, we need to add an onclick to every character, every time our game loop runs. Add this new code to your createCharacter function:

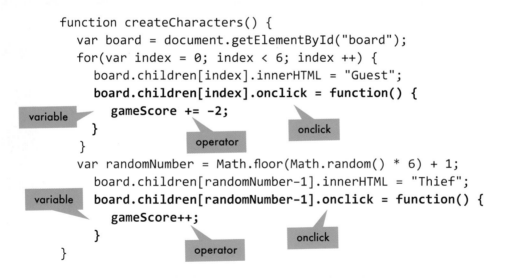

```
function createCharacters() {
    var board = document.getElementById("board");
    for(var index = 0; index < 6; index ++) {
        board.children[index].innerHTML = "Guest";
        board.children[index].onclick = function() {
            gameScore += -2;
        }
    }
    var randomNumber = Math.floor(Math.random() * 6) + 1;
        board.children[randomNumber-1].innerHTML = "Thief";
        board.children[randomNumber-1].onclick = function() {
            gameScore++;
        }
}
```

We're using the onclick, just as we did in Mission 3. When a guest or thief is created, an onclick is added. We're using two new arithmetic operators to change the value of our gameScore variable. If the user clicks on a guest, the += operator means the value that follows is added to the value in the variable. In this case, since the value that follows is -2, it means that 2 is subtracted from the gameScore value. If the user clicks on a thief, the increment operator (++) means 1 is added to the value in the variable.

5

We also need to change the alert message when the game ends, so that it tells the user their score. Change the else statement in your gameLoop function so it uses the gameScore variable value, like this:

```
function gameLoop() {
   peopleVisible = !peopleVisible;
   createCharacters();
   flashCharacters();
   loops++;
   if(loops < 12) {
      setTimeout(gameLoop, 3000);
   }
   else {
      alert("You scored " + gameScore);
   }
}
```

variable

Did you notice?

We leave a space at the end of our alert text, so the message displays correctly with the gameScore value.

 Save your HTML file and refresh your page. Try clicking on the thief every time it flashes on-screen. See how many points you score at the end of the game. Remember, you need to refresh your page before each play of the game.

Hooray! The diamond will surely be safe now!

14. Simplify the code

Now our game works, and the House of Volkov's security team can soon begin their training. But you might have noticed that our createCharacters and flashCharacters functions are quite similar. One creates our characters and the other adds a CSS class to them. We can now combine these functions to make our code simpler. Simplifying your code as you work through a problem is a really common thing to do when you're coding. It makes it much easier to understand your code.

We should change our createCharacters function so it adds the CSS class as well as creating the characters. Change the function so it looks like this:

```
function createCharacters() {
    var board = document.getElementById("board");
    var classToSet = peopleVisible ? "character visible" : "character hidden";
    for(var index = 0; index < 6; index ++) {
        board.children[index].className = classToSet;          CSS classes
        board.children[index].innerHTML = "Guest";             added
        board.children[index].onclick = function() {
            gameScore += -2;
        }
    }
    var randomNumber = Math.floor(Math.random() * 6) + 1;
    board.children[randomNumber-1].innerHTML = "Thief";
    board.children[randomNumber-1].onclick = function() {
        gameScore++;
    }
}
```

This function now does everything. Every time the game loop runs, it picks up the correct CSS class, creates the characters, and then sets the onclick for each character. We no longer need the flashCharacters function, so we can delete it. Also delete the function call from your gameLoop function, so it looks like this:

```
function gameLoop() {
    peopleVisible = !peopleVisible;
    createCharacters();          function call for
    loops++;                     flashCharacters removed
    if(loops < 12) {
        setTimeout(gameLoop, 3000);
    }
    else {
        alert("You scored " + gameScore);
    }
}
```

Save your code.
Your game will work in
exactly the same way.

Smart coding,
my friend!

180

15. Designing the game with CSS

We've got the basic structure of our game working now, but it doesn't look very fun on-screen. Let's use our CSS skills from Mission 1 to design it. First let's see if we can make our thief look more distinctive when he or she flashes up on-screen. Let's add a new CSS class called thief to our `<style>` block, like this:

```
.character {
    background-color: lightblue;
    width: 120px;
    height: 120px;
    padding: 10px;
    margin: 10px;
    float: left;
}
.thief {
    background-color: red;
}
```

Then we need to apply this CSS class to our JavaScript. Every time the thief is added, we need to add this new CSS class. To do that, we need to make this change to our code:

```
var randomNumber = Math.floor(Math.random() * 6) + 1;
board.children[randomNumber-1].innerHTML = "Thief";
board.children[randomNumber-1].onclick = function() {
   gameScore++;
}
board.children[randomNumber-1].className = classToSet + " thief";
```

 Every time our game loop runs, this will apply our thief CSS class to our thief `<div>` and make it red. Save your HTML file. Your thief will now be different from the guests.

Did you notice?

There is a space in the code " thief". This space is essential because we are using two CSS class names: the CSS class we've picked using our classToSet variable (hidden or visible), and the CSS class thief. We need the space so it doesn't end up as "hiddenthief".

16. Use images for the characters

If we want to make our character `<div>` tags look a bit more exciting, we're going to have to learn some new CSS properties. The new properties are very simple and work in exactly the same way as the ones you learned in Mission 1.

First of all, go to the *Get Coding!* website and find these two images:

Save these images with all your other HTML files in your **Coding** folder on your desktop. You've done this before in Mission 1, so go back to pages 28–30 if you need a reminder.

Guest   Thief

Now we're going to change the CSS classes in our `<style>` block. We're going to use two new CSS properties: the background and background-size CSS properties.

CSS property	What does it do?	Example values
background	Sets the background of an HTML element to an image	url('image.jpg'), none
background-size	Sets the size of the background image in an HTML element	cover, 650px

We can use these two new CSS properties in our character and thief CSS classes, like this:

```
.character {
    background: url('guest.jpg');
    background-size: cover;
    width: 120px;
    height: 120px;
    padding: 10px;
    margin: 10px;
    float: left;
}
.thief {
    background: url('thief.jpg');
    background-size: cover;
}
```

background property

background-size property

That thief's got an ugly mug!

Using the background CSS property, we ask our browser to use saved images as the background for our `<div>` tags. Then, using the background size CSS property, we ask our browser to make sure that the image file is set to a big enough size to cover the whole background of each `<div>`.

 Save your HTML file and see what the new CSS properties have done to your game.

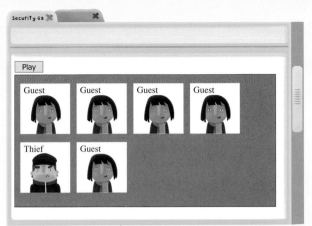

Now that we have the images set as the background of the character `<div>` tags, let's remove the guest and thief labels. After all, we don't want it to be too easy for the House of Volkov's security team. Remove the text by changing these two lines in your `<script>` block:

```
board.children[index].innerHTML = "Guest";

board.children[randomNumber-1].innerHTML = "Thief";
```

Change them to empty strings, like this:

```
board.children[index].innerHTML = "";

board.children[randomNumber-1].innerHTML = "";
```

The game is looking great!

 Save your HTML file. Now your game will just be made up of pictures.

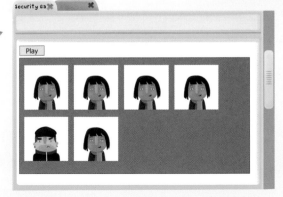

I don't like the look of that thief.

17. change the game board

Now that we know how to use the background and background-size CSS properties, we can easily change our game board background from gray to an image. Go to the *Get Coding!* website and find the background image. Save it in your **Coding** folder.

All we have to do now is add the new background and background-size properties to the board CSS class in our <style> block. Don't forget to delete the background-color CSS class, since it is no longer needed. Your code will look like this:

We should also make sure that at the start of the game, when it loads in our browser, we just see the game board. Then when we click *Play*, we see the characters. To do this, we need to add the CSS display property to the character CSS class in our <style> block, like this:

 Save your HTML file. When your game loads, you will see the new background for your game board. When you click *Play*, your characters will load on-screen and your game will begin.

```css
#board {
    background: url('background.jpg');
    background-size: cover;
    border: 1px solid black;
    height: 350px;
    width: 650px;
}
```

```css
.character {
    background: url('guest.jpg');
    background-size: cover;
    width: 120px;
    height: 120px;
    padding: 10px;
    margin: 10px;
    float: left;
    display: none;
}
```

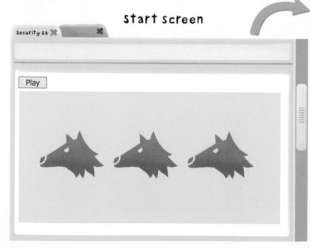

start screen

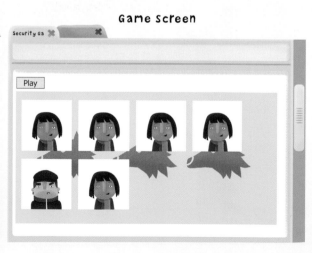

Game screen

18. Make the game harder

You might have noticed that the 3-second delay makes it easy to click on the thief. We now need to make the game harder so it's more of a challenge. The characters need to flash on-screen for a much shorter time, so there will be less time to click on the thief. To do this, we need to change the setTimeout call, like this:

```
setTimeout(gameLoop, peopleVisible ? 1000 : 3000);
```

We're using a simplified if statement, as we did earlier in the mission. We've changed our setTimeout call so that if peopleVisible is true, our gameLoop function will be called in 1 second. If peopleVisible is false, our gameLoop function will be called in 3 seconds. So now our characters will flash on-screen for only 1 second, but when they're hidden they will stay hidden for 3 seconds.

Save your code and start playing your finished game. Can you score 6 points?

Mission 5

DO-IT-YOURSELF TASK
YOUR FINISHED GAME

Coding a game is challenging, and you've mastered it in this mission. Professor Bairstone will be delighted. The game will test the security team's reaction times.

Security Training Game Brief

Check that you have correctly coded all the things below in your **securitygame.html** file and that it's saved in your **Coding** folder. Don't forget, you can change the speed of your game, making it faster and even harder for the user.

- ◆ **A game board**
- ◆ **5 guests**
- ◆ **1 thief**

- ◆ **A play button**
- ◆ **A score alert**

Turn the page to see the full code block for the game.

```
<!DOCTYPE html>
<html>
<head>
  <title>Security Game</title>
  <style>
    #board {
      background: url('background.jpg');
      background-size: cover;
      border: 1px solid black;
      height: 350px;
      width: 650px;
    }
    .character {
      background: url('guest.jpg');
      background-size: cover;
      width: 120px;
      height: 120px;
      padding: 10px;
      margin: 10px;
      float: left;
      display: none;
    }
    .thief {
      background: url('thief.jpg');
      background-size: cover;
    }
    .hidden {
      display: none;
    }
    .visible {
      display: block;
    }
  </style>
</head>
<body>
  <input type="button" value="Play" onclick="startGame()";/>
  <div id="board">
    <div class="character">1</div>
    <div class="character">2</div>
    <div class="character">3</div>
    <div class="character">4</div>
```

Mission 5 completed! Amazing work!

186

```
      <div class="character">5</div>
      <div class="character">6</div>
   </div>
   <script>
     function startGame() {
        gameLoop();
     }
     var loops = 0;
     var peopleVisible = false;
     var gameScore = 0;
     function gameLoop() {
        peopleVisible = !peopleVisible;
        createCharacters();
        loops++;
        if(loops < 12) {
           setTimeout(gameLoop, peopleVisible ? 1000 : 3000);
        }
        else {
           alert("You scored " + gameScore);
        }
     }
     function createCharacters() {
        var board = document.getElementById("board");
        var classToSet = peopleVisible ? "character visible" : "character hidden";
        for(var index = 0; index < 6; index ++) {
           board.children[index].className = classToSet;
           board.children[index].innerHTML = "";
           board.children[index].onclick = function() {
              gameScore += -2;
           }
        }
        var randomNumber = Math.floor(Math.random() * 6) + 1;
        board.children[randomNumber-1].innerHTML = "";
        board.children[randomNumber-1].onclick = function() {
           gameScore++;
        }
        board.children[randomNumber-1].className = classToSet + " thief";
     }
   </script>
</body>
</html>
```

FUTURE CODE SKILLS

This mission was an important step in learning about JavaScript game programming. You used a game loop, an essential part of nearly all computer games, to power your game and create an interactive experience for the user. This isn't an easy thing to do, so well done! You can now use your knowledge about game loops to build more complicated games that will respond to your user in different ways.

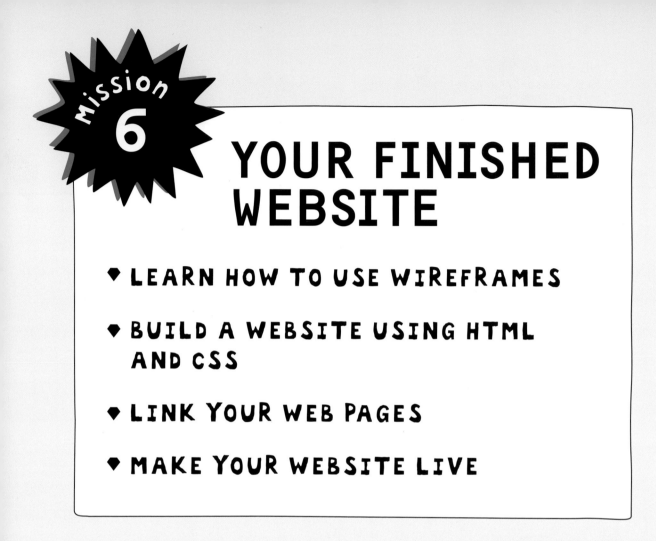

Mission 6

YOUR FINISHED WEBSITE

- ♦ LEARN HOW TO USE WIREFRAMES

- ♦ BUILD A WEBSITE USING HTML AND CSS

- ♦ LINK YOUR WEB PAGES

- ♦ MAKE YOUR WEBSITE LIVE

Dear Coder,

We think you'll be pleased to hear that the special exhibition at the House of Volkov was a resounding success! We want to thank you for all your help and hard work. When Mr. Volkov unveiled the Monk Diamond to the guests, everyone was amazed. It was the proudest moment of our careers.

The evening was not without drama, though. As we feared, the Bond Brothers had found out about the diamond. They disguised themselves as guests and used false invitations to gain access to the exhibition. Luckily, once they got inside, a member of the security team immediately noticed that they were behaving suspiciously near the diamond's glass case. Mr. Volkov intervened, and the police were called just in time. Thanks to you, the Bond Brothers are now behind bars.

The news about the Monk Diamond has spread quickly and caused quite a stir, both in Moscow and around the world. Mr. Volkov is so delighted to have it back in its rightful home that he wants to open the special exhibition to the public. Now that we know the security team is up to the challenge, we think it'll be a great show. And if people in Moscow like the exhibition, Mr. Volkov is thinking about taking it on a tour around the world. The House of Volkov has a very exciting future ahead.

There's only one thing left to do, and we thought you would like to help. Mr. Volkov needs to build a whole website (not just a web page) that will tell everyone, all over the world, about the exhibition. We hope we can rely on you one last time! Who knows? Perhaps you'll be able to come and see the Monk Diamond one day! We'd love to meet you and thank you in person.

Warmest celebratory wishes from the House of Volkov,
Professor Harry Bairstone, Dr. Ruby Day, and Ernest

P.S. Attached are Professor Bairstone's latest entry on the Explorer's Encyclopedia and a note from Mr. Volkov.

The Recovery of the Monk Diamond

From the Explorer's Encyclopedia: The Guide to Every Adventure

This entry is about the recovery of the stolen jewel. For the entry about the diamond's history, see here.

The **Recovery of the Monk Diamond** was the work of explorers Professor Harry Bairstone and Dr. Ruby Day. The pair found the diamond in the mountains of Siberia. It had been stolen from the House of Volkov in Moscow by the Bond Brothers and has now been returned.

THE EXPLORER'S ENCYCLOPEDIA
The Guide to Every Adventure

Home page
Contents
Featured discoveries
Famous explorers
Historical expeditions

VIKTOR VOLKOV
The House of Volkov, near St. Basil's Cathedral, Moscow

Dear Coder,

I just wanted to write you a short note to say thank you so much for all you have done to bring the Monk Diamond back to the House of Volkov. I was heartbroken when it was stolen, and in my darker moments I thought I would have to sell the business. The House of Volkov has been run by my family for generations, and it would have been devastating. But thanks to you, Professor Bairstone, Dr. Day, and Ernest, the Monk Diamond has been returned. I am so delighted to be hosting the exhibition and have the jewel on display in the store.

As you know, a reward was offered for its safe return or the capture of the Bond Brothers. Professor Bairstone and Dr. Day have taken their share and are going to use it to fund another expedition together. I want you to know that I also have a token of gratitude to give to you. It will be waiting for you when you come to Moscow to see the Monk Diamond for yourself.

With very warm and kind regards,
Viktor Volkov

Professor Bairstone is known for discovering ancient <u>artifacts</u> around the world. He is always accompanied on his <u>expeditions</u> by <u>Ernest</u>, his dog. Before finding the Monk Diamond, his most notable discovery was the <u>Hoy Hoard</u> of <u>Viking</u> treasure, which he unearthed on the <u>Orkney Islands</u> in <u>Scotland</u>.

Dr. Day is a scientist who studies <u>fossils</u>. She is currently researching a new species of feathered <u>dinosaur</u>. She has been on several different expeditions in the hope of discovering fossils to prove that this species had feathers.

The news of the diamond's recovery has made headlines all over the world, and the team has been interviewed by many news outlets. Professor Bairstone has been invited to give <u>lectures</u> about the discovery, and his <u>biography</u> will be published next year. Dr. Day has been made a <u>senior fellow</u> at her university.

A special exhibition featuring the recovered gem held at the House of Volkov has been very popular. Mr. Volkov told reporters he was "delighted by the return of the diamond and the success of the exhibition." Lines of up to two hours were reported, and sales have more than doubled.

BUILD A WEBSITE

You've done some great work in the last five missions. You can now code using HTML, CSS, and JavaScript and know how to use APIs to build more complex programs. You've built a web page, created a password, built a web-based app, planned a route, and built a game. Now there is one final challenge: to build a website.

So far all the pages and programs you've built have been stored in your computer's web browser and have only been for Professor Bairstone and Dr. Day to use. What we need to do now is learn how to build a website that can be accessed by anyone, anywhere in the world.

Building a website is not that different from building a web page, as we did in Mission 1. After all, a website is just a group of connected web pages. In this mission we are going to work in a slightly different way, though. This time we are going to build our web pages using a tool called a wireframe. There will be five wireframes in this mission, and you will code a web page from each one.

Wireframes

Wireframes are a useful way of planning the content and layout of a website before you start coding. Wireframes are just very simple drawings, like the example on the right, that show the different elements of your page. They help you plan out the design of each web page and make important decisions about how a page will be structured.

Wireframes also help you decide how your user will interact with the page and move among the other pages on the website. Once you are happy with your wireframe, you can then start coding, using the wireframe as a plan that shows you exactly what needs coding where on your page.

In this mission, we are going to code a website made up of five web pages. All five pages will be linked, and each will tell a different part of the diamond's exciting story. We are going to look at a possible wireframe for each page of the Monk Diamond website.

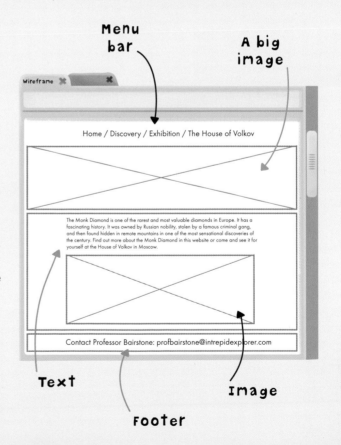

Menu bar

A big image

Home / Discovery / Exhibition / The House of Volkov

The Monk Diamond is one of the rarest and most valuable diamonds in Europe. It has a fascinating history. It was owned by Russian nobility, stolen by a famous criminal gang, and then found hidden in remote mountains in one of the most sensational discoveries of the century. Find out more about the Monk Diamond in this website or come and see it for yourself at the House of Volkov in Moscow.

Contact Professor Bairstone: profbairstone@intrepidexplorer.com

Text

Image

Footer

Let's look at the five web pages we're going to code to make the Monk Diamond website:

Web page	Content
index.html	Our home page, explaining about the discovery and exhibition
diamond.html	The history of the Monk Diamond, including the theft
discovery.html	The story of Professor Bairstone and Dr. Day's discovery
exhibition.html	The details of the exhibition, including opening times
volkov.html	How to get to the House of Volkov in Moscow

As we work through this mission, we'll look at a wireframe for each page of our website. You can then code each web page in your text-editing program using the HTML, CSS, and JavaScript skills you've learned in all the other missions.

MORE CSS PROPERTIES

In Mission 1, you learned that CSS is a programming language that lets you change the look of an HTML web page. Before we start looking at wireframes, we need to learn about a few more CSS properties and values.

USING IMAGES

When you add images to your pages, you can change their size in lots of different ways. The best way to do this is to add a style attribute to your `<img/>` tag and set the width CSS property to a value in pixels (px) or a percentage (%), like this:

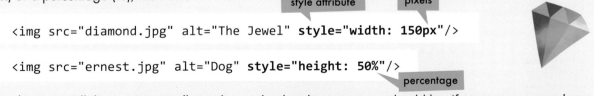

```
<img src="diamond.jpg" alt="The Jewel" style="width: 150px"/>
```

> style attribute   pixels

```
<img src="ernest.jpg" alt="Dog" style="height: 50%"/>
```

> percentage

Your browser will then automatically work out what height your image should be. If you want to stretch an image out and change its proportions, you can use both the width and height CSS properties in your style attribute, like this:

> width property   height property

```
<img src="profB.jpg" alt="Explorer" style="width: 50px; height: 50px"/>
```

Making an Image Fill a <div>

A good way to create an interesting layout is to use `<div>` tags to divide your page into different sections. If you want to use an image as the background for a `<div>` and create a banner, you should use the background and background-size CSS properties, as you did in Mission 5. There are different ways to **scale** your images using CSS properties.

CSS property	What does it do?	Example values
background	Sets the background image for an HTML element	url(filename.jpg)
background-size	Sets the size of the background of an HTML element	contain, cover, auto

In Mission 5, you used the cover value with the background-size CSS property. The cover value scales the background image so it is big enough to completely fill your `<div>`. Some of the image might be **cropped** to make it fit the size of the `<div>`.

In addition to the cover value, you can use the contain value. The contain value makes the background image as big as possible without stretching it out of shape. Depending on the size of your image, it might not fill your whole `<div>`. If the image doesn't fill the space, your browser will repeat it.

If you use auto as the value for the background-size CSS property, it will also repeat the image as many times as it needs to fill up the `<div>`.

```
<style>
  .team {
    width: 600px;
    height: 600px;
    background: url(team.jpg);
    background-size: contain;
  }
</style>
```

contain value

CODE WORDS When we **SCALE** an image, we resize it by making it bigger or smaller or giving it different proportions. When we **CROP** an image, we cut its edges off, making the image smaller.

Aligning Text and Images

You can make images and text line up in two simple ways, which we looked at in Mission 1. You can use the text-align CSS property on the `<div>` that has the text and image inside it. Or you can use the float CSS property in a style attribute inside your `<img/>` tag, like this:

float property

```
<img src="team.jpg" alt="The Team" style="float: right;"/>
```

More CSS color Values

So far you have been using color names as the values for your CSS color properties. By default, your browser supports about 140 color names. In addition to these names, you can create your own colors using a HEX code. You use a HEX code in exactly the same way you use a color name. They look like this:

HEX code

```
<body>
  <div style="background-color: #0BFF54;">
    Professor Bairstone, Dr. Day, and Ernest were on the expedition.
  </div>
</body>
```

Professor Bairstone, Dr. Day, and Ernest were on the expedition.

Luckily you don't need to remember HEX codes. There are plenty of websites that help you work them out. You can mix your own colors and make your own HEX codes using the Color Wheel at **www.color.adobe.com**. Just copy the HEX value from the page into your code and remember to start your HEX code color with a hash (#).

I can't wait to see your finished website!

1. The home page: index.html

The home page (**index.html**) is the most important page of your website because it's the page your user will see first. A good home page will make the purpose of the website obvious and engage the user's interest. It should be clear that it is only a home page and that there are other web pages on the site for the user to discover.

On our home page, let's use a big image of the Monk Diamond as the header banner for our page.

We can put a title in the banner too. Then let's have a menu bar that contains links to all the other pages on our site. Then we should have a short piece of text that explains a little bit about the Monk Diamond's discovery. Underneath the text, let's have a button that links to the House of Volkov page on the website. Finally, we can have a footer with contact details for Professor Bairstone. Let's take a look at a wireframe of this page:

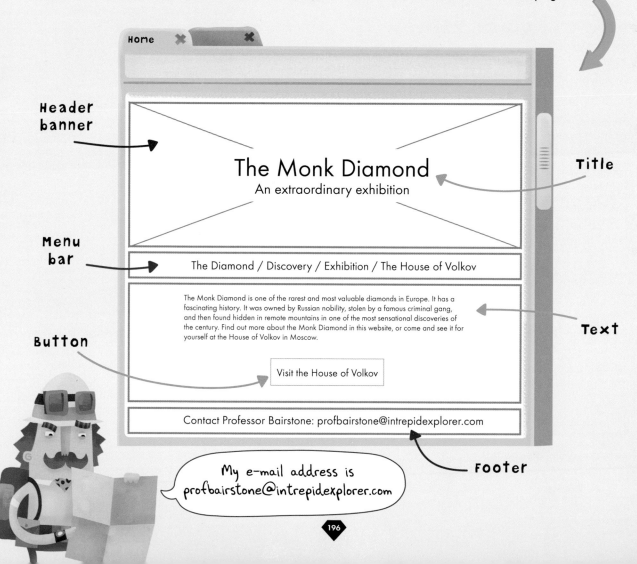

Code this page using the HTML and CSS skills you've mastered in earlier missions.

Find images of the Monk Diamond on the Get Coding! website.

Header banner

- In your `<style>` block, create a CSS class with the width property set to 100%, the height set to 400px, and the padding set to 0px. Use the background and background-size CSS properties to add an image.
- Apply this CSS class to a `<div>` in the `<body>` of your page.
- Add title text to your `<div>`. Use a style attribute to change the font-size and color CSS properties.

Menu bar

- Create a second `<div>` in the `<body>` of your page. Add a style attribute to your `<div>` tag and set the width, padding, and background-color CSS properties.
- Add four hyperlinks, using the anchor `<a>` tag and href attribute.
- You could also create a `<div>` for each link and set them to float in a horizontal line.

Text

- Create a third `<div>`, using the style attribute to set the width to 100% and the padding to 50px.
- Add your text, using the `<p>` and `<br/>` tags to divide the text into sections.

Button

- Create a button by putting a link inside a `<div>`. Use a style attribute with the width, height, padding, and background-color CSS properties to make it look like a button.

Footer

- Create a final `<div>` and use the style attribute to set the width to 100%.
- Add text inside the `<div>` with contact information for Professor Bairstone.

You can find the code for this wireframe and all the others in the mission on the Get Coding! website.

When you've finished coding your page, save your HTML file in your **Coding** folder. Call your file **index.html**.

2. The diamond page: diamond.html

The diamond page (**diamond.html**) is the second web page in our website and will tell the user all about the fascinating history of the Monk Diamond. Let's take a look at the wireframe we need to build this page:

Menu bar
♥ Create a `<div>` in the `<body>` of your page. Add a style attribute to your `<div>` tag and set the width, padding, and background-color CSS properties. Add four hyperlinks, using the anchor `<a>` tag and href attribute.
♥ You could also create a `<div>` for each link and set them to float in a horizontal line.

Big image
♥ In your `<style>` block, create a CSS class with the width property set to 100%, the height set to 200px, and the padding set to 0px. Use the background and background-size CSS properties to add an image. Apply this CSS class to a second `<div>` in the `<body>`.

Text
♥ Create a third `<div>`, using the style attribute to set the width to 100% and the padding to 50px. Add your text, using the `<p>` and `<br/>` tags to divide the text into sections.

Image
♥ Add an image inside your text `<div>`. Use the style attribute with the width, height, and text-align CSS properties to center it.

Footer
♥ Make this the same as the home page.

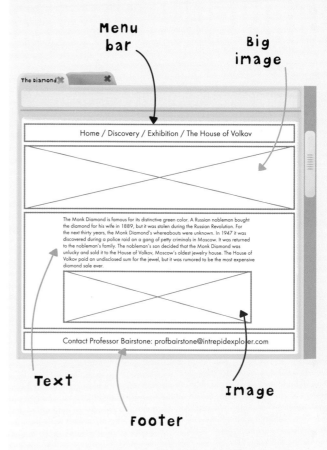

Menu bar

Big image

The Diamond

Home / Discovery / Exhibition / The House of Volkov

The Monk Diamond is famous for its distinctive green color. A Russian nobleman bought the diamond for his wife in 1889, but it was stolen during the Russian Revolution. For the next thirty years, the Monk Diamond's whereabouts were unknown. In 1947 it was discovered during a police raid on a gang of petty criminals in Moscow. It was returned to the nobleman's family. The nobleman's son decided that the Monk Diamond was unlucky and sold it to the House of Volkov, Moscow's oldest jewelry house. The House of Volkov paid an undisclosed sum for the jewel, but it was rumored to be the most expensive diamond sale ever.

Contact Professor Bairstone: profbairstone@intrepidexplorer.com

Text

Footer

Image

When you've finished coding your page, save your HTML file in your **Coding** folder. Call your file **diamond.html**.

3. The discovery page: discovery.html

The discovery page (**discovery.html**) is the third page and will tell the user how Professor Bairstone and Dr. Day found the Monk Diamond. Let's create a wireframe with a slightly different layout from our previous page, like this:

Menu bar

- This should be the same as the menu bar on the diamond page. Remember to update the links.

Big image

- In your `<style>` block, create a CSS class with the width property set to 100%, the height set to 200px, and the padding set to 0px. Use the background and background-size CSS properties to add an image. Apply this CSS class to a second `<div>` in the `<body>`.

Text column

- Create a `<div>`, using the style attribute to set the width to 80% and the padding to 50px. Add your text, using the `<p>` and `<br/>` tags to divide the text into sections.

Image column

- Create another `<div>` and use the style attribute to set the width CSS property to 20%. Float this `<div>` to the right of the `<div>` with your text in.
- Add an image inside your `<div>`. Use the style attribute with the width, height, and text-align CSS properties to center it.

Footer

- Make this the same as the home page.

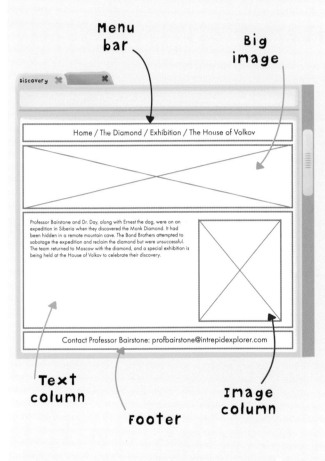

Menu bar

Big image

Discovery

Home / The Diamond / Exhibition / The House of Volkov

Professor Bairstone and Dr. Day, along with Ernest the dog, were on an expedition in Siberia when they discovered the Monk Diamond. It had been hidden in a remote mountain cave. The Bond Brothers attempted to sabotage the expedition and reclaim the diamond but were unsuccessful. The team returned to Moscow with the diamond, and a special exhibition is being held at the House of Volkov to celebrate their discovery.

Contact Professor Bairstone: profbairstone@intrepidexplorer.com

Text column

Image column

Footer

The Monk Diamond

When you've finished coding your page, save your HTML file in your **Coding** folder. Call your file **discovery.html**.

4. The exhibition page: exhibition.html

The exhibition page (**exhibition.html**) will have all the details about the exhibition at the House of Volkov. Since it contains important information, we want to keep the layout simple so the information is easy to see and understand. Let's take a look at the wireframe:

Menu bar
- This should be the same as the menu bar on the diamond and discovery pages. Just remember to update the links.

Big image
- This should also be the same as the diamond and discovery pages.

Text
- Create a `<div>` for each section of information.
- You can indent pieces of text using the style attribute and setting the CSS margin property to 10px.

Footer
- Make this the same as the home page.

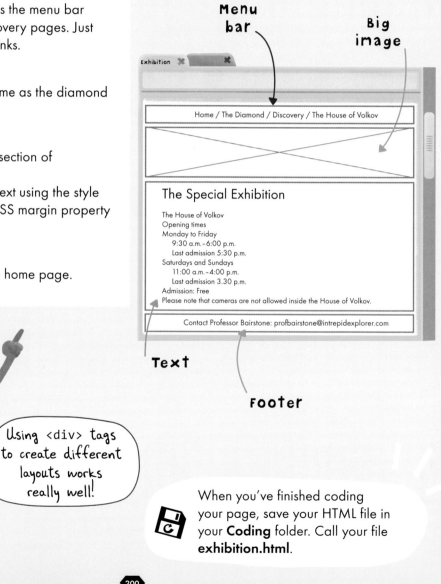

Menu bar

Big image

Exhibition

Home / The Diamond / Discovery / The House of Volkov

The Special Exhibition

The House of Volkov
Opening times
Monday to Friday
   9:30 a.m.–6:00 p.m.
   Last admission 5:30 p.m.
Saturdays and Sundays
   11:00 a.m.–4:00 p.m.
   Last admission 3.30 p.m.
Admission: Free
Please note that cameras are not allowed inside the House of Volkov.

Contact Professor Bairstone: profbairstone@intrepidexplorer.com

Text

Footer

Using `<div>` tags to create different layouts works really well!

When you've finished coding your page, save your HTML file in your **Coding** folder. Call your file **exhibition.html**.

5. The House of Volkov page: volkov.html

For the final page of our website (**volkov.html**), we need to give directions to the House of Volkov so people know where to find it. We should give the address and also embed a map from Google, using the Google Maps Embed API, as we did in Mission 4. Let's look at the wireframe:

Menu bar
- This should be the same as the menu bar on the diamond, discovery, and exhibition pages. Just remember to update the links.

Big image
- This should also be the same as the diamond, discovery, and exhibition pages.

Text column
- Create a `<div>`, using the style attribute to set the width to 80% and the padding to 50px. Add your text using the `<p>` and `<br/>` tags to divide the text into sections.

Map column
- Create another `<div>` and use the style attribute to set the width CSS property to 20%. Float this `<div>` to the right of the `<div>` with your text in.
- Add an `<iframe>` and set the width, height, and border attributes. Then add a source attribute with a URL that links to the Google Maps Embed API. Use the search API function and embed a map showing St. Basil's Cathedral in Moscow.

Footer
- Make this the same as the home page.

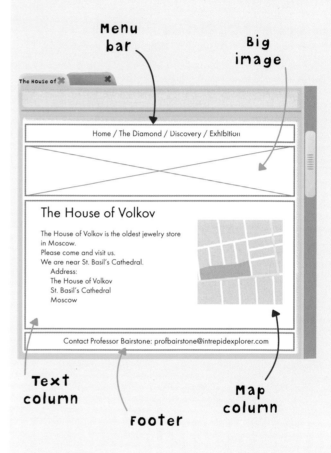

When you've finished coding your page, save your HTML file in your **Coding** folder. Call your file **volkov.html**.

YOUR FINISHED WEBSITE

Now that you've built your five web pages, the final thing you need to do is make sure that all your links are correct and that your pages connect in the way you had planned. Check that the menu bar on each of your web pages has the correct file name in each of the links. If your links aren't right, your website won't work, because the user won't be able to navigate between the pages. Your code for each link will look like this:

```
<a href="index.html">Home</a>
<a href="diamond.html">The Diamond</a>
<a href="discovery.html">Discovery</a>
<a href="exhibition.html">Exhibition</a>
<a href="volkov.html">The House of Volkov</a>
```

Making Your Own Wireframes

Making your own wireframes is very easy. Lots of people just use a pencil, piece of paper, and sticky notes to do it, drawing a wireframe that shows what their website will look like before they start to code. This is sometimes called paper **prototyping**. It's a really quick way to experiment with your layouts before you spend time coding them up.

If you want to make wireframes like the ones we've used here, there are plenty of tools available. You can use Microsoft Visio on a PC, Gliffy and Balsamiq mock-ups in a web browser, or OmniGraffle if you're on a Mac. All these programs come with premade graphics that you can use to quickly sketch out your pages on a computer.

CODE WORDS A **PROTOTYPE** is the first version of an object. The prototype is used to see what needs to be changed and improved in later versions and the finished object.

That's the final mission accomplished!

Making Your Website Live

If you want other people to see your finished website, you need to upload it to a web server. At the beginning of the book, we learned about web servers. They can be hardware or software, and they store websites so your web browser can access them. For people to be able to see your website, you need to **host** it on a web server on the Internet. Setting up your own web server is complicated, so luckily there are lots of online companies that will let you use their servers to host your files.

CODE WORDS When a web server stores a website so web browsers can access it, we say the server **HOSTS** the website. When files are hosted by a server, they'll have a URL (web address), just like all the other websites on the Internet.

Did you know?

If you want to host your files, you should ask an adult for help to look for web space on a server. Just as with a Google account, you have to be a certain age to sign up.

If you want to find a free web server to host your website, there are lots to choose from on the Internet. Just search for "free web hosting." Sometimes home Internet connections come with web space that you can use. Once you have a web host, you'll have to copy your files to their server. Carefully read the instructions and terms and conditions that your web host gives you.

Great work! We beat the Bond Brothers and safely returned the Monk Diamond to Mr. Volkov!

And we're famous!

WHAT NEXT?
YOUR CODING FUTURE

Over the six missions in this book, you have not only kept the Monk Diamond safe from the Bond Brothers, but have also learned all about HTML, CSS, and JavaScript. You've coded a web page, made a password, built a web-based app, planned a route, and mastered some very complicated code to build a game. And now you can add creating a website to your achievements. Congratulations!

We hope *Get Coding!* has shown you how fun and interesting coding can be. You've learned a truly impressive number of new Code Skills and built some exciting projects of your own. And there's still much, much more to learn. If you enjoyed coding in HTML and CSS, there are plenty of other HTML tags and CSS attributes that you can learn about from lots of excellent websites on the Internet.

The W3Schools HTML site, which can be found at **www.w3schools.com/html**, will guide you through plenty of examples so you can expand your knowledge and make even more exciting websites.

If you enjoyed coding in JavaScript, why not sharpen up your skills by working through some of the exercises available on sites like Codecademy, at **www.codecademy.com/learn/javascript**?

Or you could start learning new programming languages for coding programs that run outside your browser. Why not try learning C#, Java, or Ruby? Or try your hand at coding your own web servers? Take a look at **www.code.org/learn** for more ideas.

And finally, don't forget to join the Young Rewired State community. We will help you to keep developing your coding skills and be a technology star of the future!

The *Get Coding!* missions have been a great success. It's up to you where you go next.

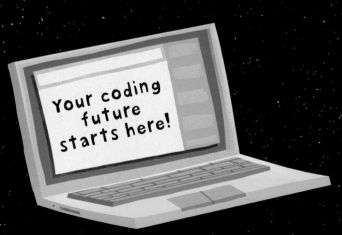
Your coding future starts here!

Joining Young Rewired State

Join Young Rewired State and we will introduce you to like-minded people and expert mentors at free events all over the world, like our Festival of Code. Through us you will learn how to build apps, websites, and algorithms and be inspired to use your skills to solve real-world challenges.

Young
Rewired
State_

Find out more about Young Rewired State:
www.yrs.io   www.getcodingkids.com

INDEX

alternative (alt) attribute 28
anchor <a> tag 62–63
appendChild method 108–111
Application Program Interfaces (APIs) 103
    API key 139–141
    math API 177
    web APIs 138–141
apps (applications) 7
    web-based 98–133
attributes 27–28, 32, 34, 48, 82–85, 88, 101–102,
        142–144

background property 182–183, 194
background-color property 36–37
background-size property 182–183, 194
body <body> tag 21
border property 43
buttons 98–100, 112–113

camelCase 67
class attributes 48
code blocks 56–57, 92, 132–133, 151, 174–175, 186–187
Code Skills 23, 26, 29–30, 33, 37, 44–45, 50–52, 63, 65,
        70–71, 74, 76, 81, 85, 100, 102, 107, 110–111,
        116–117, 120, 122–124, 126–127, 140–141, 144,
        147, 160–161, 169
color property 39, 195
computers 6
createElement method 108–111
cropping 194
CSS (Cascading Style Sheets) 10
    classes 46–48, 50–54
    coding 34–54
    measurements 41–42

properties 34–45, 168–169, 182–183, 193–195
using with JavaScript 172
values 34, 193–195

display property 168–169
division <div> tag 32–33
Do-It-Yourself Tasks 55, 91, 131, 150, 185
<!DOCTYPE> declaration 21
Document Object Model (DOM) 103–124
    methods and properties 104–111, 118–120

element selector 53–54
else statements 75–76
embedded content 138, 142–147
empty strings 172

float property 40

game building 156–187
getElementById method 105–107
Google Maps 139–141, 145–149

head <head> tag 21, 46
height property 41–42
HEX codes 195
href attribute 62–63
home pages 196–197
hosting 203
HTML (HyperText Markup Language) 10
    coding 20–33
    document 9
    elements 9, 10, 103, 104–111, 118–124
    tags 10, 20–30, 142–144
    using with JavaScript 82–90

HTML5 localStorage 125–130
hyperlinks 62–65, 84

id attribute 87
id selector 157
if statements 72–74
inline frame <iframe> tag 142–144
image <img/> tag 27–30, 193–194
innerHTML property 105–107
input <input/> tag 87–88, 98–102
Internet 8–9

JavaScript 10
  coding 66–93
  functions 78–81, 101–102, 159–161
  operators 69–72, 166
  statements 67, 72–76
  using with CSS 172
  using with HTML 82–90
  variables 68, 70–71
JPEG 27

line break <br/> tag 25, 26
loops 130, 162–163, 166–167, 170–171, 176

margin property 43

onclick attribute 82–85, 101–102

padding property 43
paragraph <p> tag 24, 26
passwords 86–93
percentages 42
pixels 38, 41
points 41
programming languages 7, 10
programs 6
prototypes 202

removeChild method 118–120
reserved words 83

scale 194
script <script> tag 66
self-closing tag 25

software 6
source (src) attribute 27
string parameters 145–146
style attribute 32, 34
style <style> tag 47
syntax 35

text box 98–100, 112–114
text-align property 39
text-editing programs 14
title <title> tag 21
type attribute 88
type attribute selector 99

URLs 9
  image URLs 28

web addresses. See URLs
web browsers 8–9
web pages 8, 9, 23, 55–57
  linking 64–65
web servers 9, 203
websites 8, 64–65, 192–203
width property 41–42
wireframes 192, 202
World Wide Web 8

With thanks to
David Whitney, Ruth Nicholls,
Emma Mulqueeny, and the
Young Rewired State ambassadors:
Alexander Craggs, Michael Cullum,
Chloe Gutteridge, Ross Kelso,
Stephen Mount, James Thompson,
Hugh Wells

First U.S. edition 2017

Library of Congress Catalog Card Number pending
ISBN 978-0-7636-9833-1 (hardcover)
ISBN 978-0-7636-9276-6 (paperback)

17 18 19 20 21 22 LEO 10 9 8 7 6 5 4 3 2 1

Printed in Heshan, Guangdong, China

This book was typeset in Futura and Bokka.
The illustrations were created digitally.

Candlewick Press
99 Dover Street
Somerville, Massachusetts 02144

visit us at www.candlewick.com